PROMISES FULFILLED AND UNFULFILLED IN MANAGEMENT EDUCATION

REFLECTIONS ON THE ROLE, IMPACT AND FUTURE
OF MANAGEMENT EDUCATION: EFMD PERSPECTIVES,
VOLUME 1

PROMISES FULFILLED AND UNFULFILLED IN MANAGEMENT EDUCATION

BY

HOWARD THOMAS

*Lee Kong Chian School of Business, Singapore Management
University, Singapore*

LYNNE THOMAS

Visual Counselling and Coaching, Stratford-on-Avon, UK

ALEXANDER WILSON

*Singapore Management University, Singapore;
Loughborough University, UK*

United Kingdom – North America – Japan
India – Malaysia – China

Emerald Group Publishing Limited
Howard House, Wagon Lane, Bingley BD16 1WA, UK

First edition 2013

Copyright © 2013 Emerald Group Publishing Limited

Reprints and permission service
Contact: permissions@emeraldinsight.com

British Library Cataloguing in Publication Data
A catalogue record for this book is available from the British Library

ISBN: 978-1-78190-714-6

ISOQAR certified
Management Systems,
awarded to Emerald for
adherence to Quality
and Environmental
standards ISO 9001:2008
and 14001:2004,
respectively

Certificate Number 1985
ISO 9001
ISO 14001

INVESTOR IN PEOPLE

To: The Thomas family and the Wilson family who are the foundation of our lives.

Contents

Acknowledgements

This book would not have been completed without the collaboration and help of a number of key people.

To Eric Cornuel and Matthew Wood of EFMD we owe our immeasurable gratitude for encouraging Howard and Lynne Thomas to undertake the research work which informs the content of this book. They have also offered constant encouragement and support throughout the research and writing phases of this volume.

We wish to thank the 39 individuals listed in the appendix who gave us two to three hours of their time and were highly supportive, open and frank in answering our questions. Their professionalism, expertise and willingness to share their viewpoints increased the depth and quality of the insights about management education presented here.

We also owe a huge debt of gratitude to colleagues in Singapore Management University, particularly Professor Arnoud de Meyer, who have provided the stimuli and enthusiasm to push this project through to fruition. In particular our sincere appreciation goes to Susan Chong Oi Yin (HT's deputy PA at SMU) for cheerfully and professionally executing the typing and revision of various excellent drafts of the book; to Gillian Goh Cheng Cheng for outstanding research assistance; to Michelle Lee Pui Yee (Associate Professor of Marketing at SMU) for coordinating the research assistants and offering sound advice and, finally to Dorasen Khoo Ban Yie (HT's PA at SMU) for her constant encouragement and organization of HT's time.

As authors we would like to acknowledge the financial and academic support offered by SMU and particularly to Alex Wilson who visited SMU, LKCSB as Lim Kim Son Research Fellow in Strategy and Organisation in Summer 2011 and Summer 2012. We also appreciate the help, and advice of Michael Thomas, Blue-eyed Digital Marketing UK and David Thomas, Highwire DTC, Lancaster University UK.

Finally, the quality and exposition of the written argument, has been considerably improved by the excellent and tireless efforts of George Bickerstaffe, the Consultant Editor of EFMD. We are extremely grateful to him for his professionalism and expertise but recognize that we alone are responsible for the content and structuring of the argument in the book.

— Howard Thomas, Lynne Thomas and Alexander Wilson

Foreword: Setting the Scene

This book had its conception in conversations between the lead author and Eric Cornuel, the distinguished Director General and CEO of The European Foundation for Management Development (EFMD) in Brussels. Eric was looking for a way to mark the 40th anniversary of EFMD in 2012, perhaps reflecting and building on the volume of reflections on management education, *Training the Fire Brigade*, which celebrated EFMD's 25th anniversary.

After some intensive discussions it was decided that I would produce a book based on interviews with a broad range of leaders and stakeholders in management education about the past and future of the sector. During 2011 and 2012 a total or 39 face-to-face semi-structured but largely open-ended interviews lasting two to three hours were conducted. Our deepest respect and admiration for their patience and perseverance goes to these respondents.

Their responses have been interpreted and analysed by the research team. Such was the richness and depth of their insights that the book has been divided into two volumes.

Volume 1 focuses on the past performance of management education particularly over the years since the publication of *Training the Fire Brigade* and the lessons learned and not learned over the last 20 years or so (focusing on both the positives and negatives). Volume 2 takes up the theme of change and reviews the need for transformation and the future direction of the evolution of management education.

Foreword: Eric Cornuel

Welcome to this special publication from the European Foundation for Management Development (EFMD). In the following pages you will find one of the most comprehensive, credible and coherent analyses of the current state of management education, not just in Europe but also around the world.

Management education is, of course, a key raison d'être of EFMD and the publication of *Promises Fulfilled and Unfulfilled in Management Education: Reflections on the Role, Impact and Future of Management Education: EFMD Perspectives* by Howard Thomas, Lynne Thomas and Alexander Wilson in part marks and celebrates the 40th anniversary of EFMD's foundation. I am convinced that management education will be a key element in our global recovery from a crisis that has proved to be unprecedentedly deep and long-lived.

Promises Fulfilled and Unfulfilled does not always share that conviction but I remain optimistic. The very fact that the management education 'industry' can examine so openly and forensically the challenges it faces and it's own shortcomings only reassures me that it will ultimately respond positively and with eventual success.

My enormous thanks goes out to Howard, Lynne and Alexander for their exceptional work in putting the book together. I would like to also thank the 39 willing interviewees who gave so generously of their time and insights.

My final thanks is reserved whole-heartedly for EFMD and the network. EFMD is a truly unique network of members at the heart of one of the most important aspects of society and your continued support and commitment to EFMD now, and over the past 40 years is an inspiration to us all.

Eric Cornuel
Director General and CEO, EFMD

Chapter 1

Introduction: EFMD's Journey in Management Education

In 1996 a special jubilee volume outlined the evolution and history of the European Foundation for Management Development (EFMD) and sought to identify some of the key issues that had driven management education over 25 years (1971–1996). The volume comprised a series of essays by experts in the management education field that allowed the writers to explore the future of management education against the economic and political backdrop of the European environment.

Ray Van Schaik (1996, p. 14), the then president of EFMD, suggested that 'one of the most fundamental properties (of business schools) will be that their students will know how to handle the unexpected, how to handle life'. He went on to add that 'on top of technical skills — which have become a *sine qua non* ... new managers more than ever should abhor rigid concepts and thrive on the art of improvisation'.

Schaik also clearly specified his vision for the role and purpose of EFMD in the management education environment:

> It should endeavour to continue to be a *trait d'union*, a link, between the corporate world and the world of education; it should continue to build and explore a network of personal and business relationships that enables it to contribute to the process of high-quality, practical, "true to life" education ... and finally, it should continue to cement its relationship with governments and public bodies that are involved in the process of management and education.

Indeed, it is clear that the positioning of the European business school has been strongly influenced and shaped by the strategic role of EFMD since its founding in 1971. EFMD has constantly focused on linking European experience and ideas with management practice and learning. It has also emphasised internationalisation and corporate linkages as essential to high-quality management education.

By the early 1990s it was clear that European business schools had gained respect and growing influence. Indeed, Professor Pedro Nueno, trained at Harvard Business School and a European pioneer at IESE (Barcelona), EFMD and CEIBS (Shanghai), and Claude Rameau,[1] a former dean of INSEAD, noted that the diversity, identity and internationalism of Europe and European management should be an inspiration for the rest of the world. They believed that EFMD and European management schools should emphasise their international character and be agents for transformation and change in management education.

The record of EFMD demonstrates its continued commitment to international linkages and activities. In part, this outward-looking propensity is born out of the lessons of history. Europe has always been witness to an interplay and exchange of cultures, arising from trade, colonial empires and the strong international influences of such countries as the UK (in Commonwealth countries), France (in South-east Asia and North Africa), the Netherlands (in Africa) and Spain/Portugal (in the Americas). It is also amplified by the more recent importance of the EU as an economic and trading union that is a significant element in the global economy.

For example, during the first 25 years of its existence the International Programmes Unit of EFMD promoted a range of international alliances and research centres including Euro-China, Euro-India, Euro-CIS, Euro-Arab and Euro-Palestine. This unusually wide-ranging international footprint attests to both influences acting on it and its own pioneering intent to transform the educational infrastructure of rapidly emerging economies such as China and India through co-operation with experts from European schools.

The Euro-China initiative, for example, led directly to the establishment of the first independent international business school in China (CEIBS — the China-European International Business School) in 1994. With subsequent investment this school is now a very significant, and important, Asian school with broad international recognition in the rankings.

Fragueiro and Thomas (2011) provide a comprehensive 'map' of the management education landscape in Europe, showing the breadth of the marketplace and its heterogeneous nature. They point out that European schools generally are viewed as eclectic and flexible and to have generated a range of academic and business models reflecting their different leadership styles and cultural influences.

---

1. See 'Training the Fire Brigade', EFMD Publications, 1996 (p. 57).

Almost every country in Europe now has a set of national business school champions and many are internationally ranked. France, the UK, Spain and Switzerland have probably led the growth of international schools, though other countries, such as Germany, are now producing an increasingly important set of business schools.

What then are the characteristics of European management schools? What makes them distinctive?

1.1. Is There a Distinctive, European Management Model?

It is argued in the EFMD (1996) volume and in Thomas (2012) that the European identity and model of management education have been shaped by a range of environmental characteristics that differentiate the European scene.[2]

- As noted already, Europe and the EU is a large trading area involving many cultures and countries. Its diversity means that European trading corporations have learned how to expand and develop their businesses across borders. They have wide experience of international business and international relations.
- European companies have grown in size and have become leaner and fitter through European and international competition. As a consequence a series of large influential multi-national European corporations has emerged and gained reputation in the marketplace.
- Most European countries have a strong governmental and public-sector influence on the conduct of business and business policy. Europeans tend to accept and recognise a broader role for government in business and society.
- Europeans generally favour socially responsible capitalism over what is sometimes unkindly characterised as unbridled market capitalism. Centrist models of social democracy are more common in the European political environment than in the United States.

As a result, European business, and European management education, has developed a balanced relationship with government and society. In this context, business grows not only economically and technically but also with social responsibility and legitimacy. The European culture and environment encourage more direct co-operation with government to improve poverty

---

2. See also Phillipe de Woot in 'Training the Fire Brigade' (EFMD, 1996, p. 151).

and social welfare with an emphasis on balanced human and economic progress.

As a result of contextual and cultural differences in European management education the following themes, and differentiating features, are also evident:

- The belief in socially responsible management education as stressed by agencies such as the GRLI (Globally Responsible Leaders Initiative), EABIS (European Academy for Business in Society) and PRME (Principles for Responsible Management Education), which have been carefully nurtured by EFMD.
- The development of close linkages between business schools and corporate organisations and the consequent strong bridges between management education and practice fuelled a rapid expansion of executive education in Europe. This has led to a focus on action-based project-oriented learning, often providing clear evidence of promising management practices in business.
- Internationalisation and globalisation are very important to large European corporations (and the EU as a trading bloc) as they expand their markets and corporate influence globally. European schools such as INSEAD (in Singapore and, more recently, Abu Dhabi), Nottingham (in China) and CEIBS (in Shanghai) provide evidence of how European schools have rapidly built an international footprint to mirror the international growth perspectives of European businesses.
- The Bologna Process and European Accord in management education have also considerably strengthened European management education through the creation of common structures for degree-level management education. The resulting simple credit transfer process across courses taken in different European management education institutions has strongly facilitated co-operation and network building among these institutions.
- EFMD'S EQUIS business school accreditation process (started in 1997) demonstrates its strong emphasis on high-quality management education. The CLIP programme shows a similar emphasis on quality assurance in corporate and executive education.
- There is currently a much greater emphasis on cross-European educational networking for the development of interdisciplinary research programmes and high-quality faculty development. Thus, the quality of European research output is well recognised on the world scene.

It can be argued that European management educators have adopted a more balanced, and somewhat less analytically rigorous, perspective on management education than is common in, for example, the United States.

They often believe in a closer linkage with practice and focus on a balanced view of management and leadership.

Paul Danos (2011), dean of Tuck Business School at Dartmouth College in the United States, expresses it in the following terms in discussing the philosophy of IE (Instituto de Empresa) in Madrid and its dean, Santiago Iniguez: 'His is a world where the professor is a teacher first, and the weight of research and practical experience in that teaching depends on each situation. That contrasts with the classic US model where research professors are seen as the prime teaching asset, and research itself fosters expertise about the world of practice'.

Europeans tend to view formal analytic and strategy models and technical skills as valuable and sensible but also argue that such analytically rigorous approaches may be too heavily emphasised in current curricula. This, in turn, may lead to the production of scientific research of little practical managerial relevance.

As noted by Schaik (1996), an emphasis on softer skills, more socially responsible management, and vision and communication skills for engaging employees are viewed as critical and important. Indeed, Europeans believe strongly in a balanced philosophy in management education involving an appropriate mix of course and project work to develop skills of analysis, synthesis and criticism. Through this process, the differentiation between European and other models of management education becomes clear and provides welcome diversity in models of management education.

1.2. The Approach Taken in this Volume

We decided to adopt a different research-oriented approach for this 40th anniversary volume. Following discussions with Eric Cornuel and Matthew Wood of EFMD, we drew upon the foundations of the 1996 volume to frame our research design and questionnaire. Through an open-ended interview research process, we sought to explore the perspectives and views of a wide range of experts drawn not only from the European environment but also from the United States and other global players in management education. To inform the structure of the questions posed and the research design, we also listened to the views of deans who attended meetings of EFMD and AACSB in Vienna and Tampa in the United States in 2010 with the objective of gauging the nature of current business school debates.

The deans consulted (Schlegelmilch & Thomas, 2011) singled out three broad areas of interest: soft skills, ethics and CSR, and globalisation. There was also a belief that the link to practice, and the wider social community, needs to be strengthened.

They also stressed that there are an increasingly complex and inter-dependent set of global problems (e.g. global competition, global sourcing, global financing and global customers) that require the production of managers possessing global cultural and contextual intelligence, under-standing and sensitivity. We, therefore, added an exploration of some of these issues in the questionnaire.

In order to gain insight into experts' views, both retrospectively and prospectively, on the key issues, events, challenges and opportunities in management education, we identified and approached interview participants with different roles and viewpoints. We believe that understanding the relations and interactions between the various actors in management education is fundamental to our analysis of the roles, value and purpose of management education.

The research is based on a series of in-depth interviews conducted across a set of influential stakeholders to develop a more comprehensive and informed view about management education and its evolution. We conducted nearly 40 interviews (39 in total) lasting between two and three hours, taking in the expert views of stakeholders from academia, professional bodies, media and business (the appendix has the interviewees and their affiliations). Each of these interviews, which were tape-recorded and subsequently transcribed with the consent of the interviewees, followed a semi-structured design to guide key thematic areas and to allow respondents the flexibility, and spontaneity to expand on issues they found relevant and important to the discussion. Interviewees were asked to focus on the time period from EFMD's formation in 1971 to the present and also to consider likely future scenarios for management education.

From the research we subsequently draw insights about the culture and context of management education in terms of its current and future profile. The plan for the rest of Volume 1 is as follows:

1. Chapter 2 gives a brief overview of the broad history and evolution of management education from its emergence in the late 19th century to the present, when it has come under intense criticism following the global financial crisis and a series of corporate scandals that highlight an apparent lack of any corporate moral and ethical compass.
2. Chapter 3 parallels the evolution of management education with a detailed evaluation of the history and development of the EFMD over the last 40 years. Using a timeline of milestones and significant EFMD activities over the period, we examine not only the challenges and issues identified by experts in the 1996 volume but also provide a review of the themes identified in the academic and media literature about manage-ment education. These observations are then compared with the challenges identified by respondents in our research. How far have these

changed? One issue that is clear from Chapter 2 is the increasing range and influence of stakeholder viewpoints about, and influences on, management education.

3. Chapter 4 examines the stakeholder management perspective (which we call the 'stakeholder spring') in management education. It focuses, through the results of the research, on important stakeholder issues such as who and what are the most significant and important influences on management education.
4. Chapters 5 and 6 map the stakeholder views of key events, innovations and role models in management education over the last 20 years. Are there, for example, new or distinctive, business models in management education? Do particular institutions or their leaders have a strong influence?
5. Chapter 7 then examines the different stakeholder perspectives on lessons learned and questions whether the promise of management education has been fulfilled.
6. Chapter 8 discusses change in management education specifically and the barriers to, and the potential triggers for, change. The afterword then transitions the volume to the context of the future of management education, the subject of Volume 2.

Chapter 2

A Brief Overview of the Emergence and Evolution of Management Education and the Business School

2.1. Introduction

Without doubt business schools have been one of the success stories of higher education over the last 50 years. As Noorda (2011, p. 520) says: 'In many aspects business schools are perfect proof of what you get when universities are doing what they are supposed to do and doing it well. They are fit for purpose because they are serving the specific needs of the communities they relate to'.

Even so, over the last 10 years the business school has come under intense critical fire (e.g. Jacobs, 2009) over its legitimacy as a serious, academic discipline (e.g. Nussbaum, 1997) and over its failure to reach its original ambitious goal of the professionalisation of management (e.g. Khurana, 2007). Yet, while business schools have failed to turn management into a profession, they have been somewhat more successful in recasting it as a science (Schlegelmilch & Thomas, 2011, p. 478) even though Mintzberg (2004, 2009) argues that management is in fact neither a science nor a profession but rather an art or craft.

It is clear that management education currently has both an image problem and an identity crisis. Therefore, it is important to review the following issues as necessary background to our research into the performance of management education:

1. To present a broad overview of the historical development of the modern business school and management education
2. To examine the current intense criticism of business and business schools and identify its key features and issues
3. To reflect on the core issues that have risen to the surface and are perceived to be persistent problems in management education.

2.2.   The Evolution of Management Education and the 'Business School' Concept

Four countries — France, Germany, the United Kingdom and the United States — have been prominent catalysts in the growth of management education from the 19th century to the present day. Their common initial focus was to educate managers in the practical aspects of management. The French called their management education schools 'Ecoles de Commerce', the Germans 'Handelschochschulen', the British 'Schools of Commerce' and the Americans 'Business Schools'.

The evolution of business schools features a number of key milestones *en route* to the present somewhat confused state of affairs. (Table 2.1, drawn from the lead author's previous work, identifies five phases or generations in the evolution of the business school.)

In the initial emergence stage, the 'trade-school' era, in the late 19th to the early 20th century, the original purpose of management education centred on the idea of a liberal and moral education for business people. The aim was to enhance the status of the professional manager in public and private life. (Moldoveanu & Martin, 2008, describes it as 'Business 1.0')

Pioneer schools, such as the Wharton School (founded in 1881 and influenced by the founder Joseph Wharton and Frederick Taylor's scientific management principles) and Harvard Business School (founded in 1908), became the catalysts of future growth (phase 2). Along with the development of complementary assets such as textbooks, curricula and case studies, the founding of AACSB (the American Association for Collegiate Schools of Business) in 1916 closely followed the growth of the new business schools. However, these schools did little, or no, research and were seen as 'wastelands of vocationalism'.

The Gordon/Howell (Ford/Carnegie Foundation sponsored) reports in the United States in the late 1950s were therefore charged with examining the claim that business schools lacked research output, academic credibility and legitimacy. The conclusions of these reports proposed an alternative business school model that emphasised strong social science perspectives and academic rigour (this is phase 3 in our model or 'Business 2.0' in Moldoveanu & Martin's term). The educational philosophy of logical positivism embodied discipline-led scholarship with a clear focus on analytical models and scientific rigour. This US model together with a redesigned general management MBA degree became the dominant design for business schools in the 1960s and 1970s.

However, by the late 1970s and early 1980s concerns began to emerge from practitioners and academics about the overly scientific focus of business schools and the lack of relevance to real-life management issues of

Table 2.1: Evolution of business schools as a social construction process.

Generation and time period	Behavioural characteristics and causes	Implications and consequences	Legitimacy providers
First generation (19th century–early 20th century) Emergence of alternative business school models 'Trade School' Vocational Era	Different knowledge structures, frames of reference and cognitive maps Different beliefs about management education but mainly vocational trade-type models focusing on commercial and administrative practice	Beliefs about market boundaries vary across countries Differential rates of growth and adoption across countries Influence of culture, regulations, country characteristics and languages evident at local and national level Size of schools tends to be nationally determined	• The creation of managerial employment by industrialists, entrepreneurial individuals and the state to cope with larger organisations • Institutionalised managerial systems, e.g. accounting practices • Establishment of AACSB (1916) and subsequent accreditation systems for business schools
Second generation (early 20th century–1970s) Clearly shaped national schools	Strategic reference points established in countries — US model is key reference point Imitative behaviour at a local/national level The image and identity of a business school becomes clear Institutionalising processes	The identification of national role models and a dominant industry recipe means that differences exist among the key drivers of • Governance • Funding and endowment • International mindset • Innovation	• National governments • Universities • 'Feeder' disciplines (economics, psychology)

Table 2.1: (*Continued*)

Generation and time period	Behavioural characteristics and causes	Implications and consequences	Legitimacy providers
		• Knowledge transmission • Corporate linkages	
Third generation (1970s–1990s) Dominance of US business school model Growing strength of national champions	Industry recipe is established—dominant design/role model is evident Reputational structures and clear identities formed Internationalising processes Organisational adaptation and interpretation Benchmarking processes	Issues of image and reputation become important Social capital is built-up long-term Rankings and league tables become indicators of success International alliances form to enhance reputations of leading schools in the United States and Europe	• Research rankings and citations • Globalised performance measures and rankings • National performance measures • International accreditation bodies (e.g. AACSB, EFMD, AMBA)
Fourth generation (1990–2005) Strong emergence of European business school model	• Mounting criticism of US business school model • European industry recipe is established (mimicry of US model challenged) • Emphasis on internationalisation and public management • Clear European identity sought (e.g. EU)	Recipe includes • Largely one year MBA model • Strong executive education focus • Push for softer skills and linkages to the role of business and government in society • Competing on high-quality research as per US model but	EU The Bologna accord in higher education (common degree structures and credit transfer) Role of EFMD • Founding of EQUIS Accreditation system as European accreditation

Fifth generation (2005–Present) Strong range of global models Globalisation in emerging markets (Asia, Eastern Europe, Latin America)	• Shift of global economy from west to east • Increasing criticism and blame attached to business schools for the global financial crisis (teaching ambassadors of market capitalism) • Issues of ethics, corporate social responsibility and sustainability become central to business schools • Questioning of market capitalism — search for a	• Executive education and corporate relevance/linkages important • Strong decline of state funding of higher education in general and management education in particular • Strong reputations/identities developed for European schools INSEAD, IMD, LBS etc. • Little private/endowment funding	• Adaptation of the business school models to different cultures, and political and economic systems • Clear strategic reference points (business schools) emerge • CEIBS (Shanghai) • FUDAN (China) • HKUST (Hong Kong) • NUS (Singapore) • GETULIO VARGAS (Brazil) • IIM (India)	• strong focus on impactful research • INSEAD opens campus in Singapore — slogan 'The Business School for the World'. Other schools follow international expansion approach • EFMD launches CEIBS as a business school in Shanghai in partnership with City of Shanghai	CEEMAN develops accreditation for schools in Eastern Europe Increasing number of business school associations • CLADEA (Latin America) • AAPBS (Asia Pacific) • AIMS (India) Role of EABIS (Europe) PRME/GLRI (EFMD) UN Global Compact and Aspen Institute in promoting ethical/societal values	High rankings for European schools (HEC, IESE, IMD, INSEAD, LBS) in *FT* rankings

Table 2.1: (*Continued*)

Generation and time period	Behavioural characteristics and causes	Implications and consequences	Legitimacy providers
	broader stakeholder view of management • Influence of governments in Asia on business school development very strong (e.g. Singapore, Hong Kong, China)	• ISB (India) • IEDC (Slovenia) • Skolkovo (Moscow) • Continued questioning of the role and purpose of Business Schools • Is it a professional school? • Alternative models?	Strong ranking of Asian schools (CEIBS, HKUST and ISB) in *FT* rankings

Sources: Fragueiro and Thomas (2011); Thomas and Wilson (2011).

much academic management research. Notable academic critics included Professors Hayes, Abernathy, Levitt and Livingston at Harvard Business School. They argued that despite all efforts there was still no established body of managerial knowledge. Whether as a result of this or not, the field of management education suddenly saw an explosion of readable management books from authors such as Jim Collins, Gary Hamel, Tom Peters and Michael Porter (some management academics, some management consultants). These books told, through the vehicle of cases and well-constructed stories, how managers and leaders addressed and handled strategic issues such as competition, diversification and organisational change. They helped to bridge the gap between academic research and managerial relevance and had strong appeal to the growing generation of managers and leaders.

At the same time European schools such as HEC (France), IESE (Spain), IMD (Switzerland), INSEAD (France) and LBS (United Kingdom) established their growing influence on management education and established an European identity (phase 4 of our model).

They stressed elements that were more reflective of European traditions including action-learning, practice-engaged research, customised executive education and, most importantly, a focus on international linkages, activities and research. A distinctly European identity and style in management education was apparent. And in the last 10 years (phase 5 of our model) this has been joined by a rapidly evolving Asian identity and form of business school following the shift in the global economy from west to east.

Nevertheless, criticism of business schools and management education has continued unabated. The conventional judgement is that the business school model is definitely in transition and business schools are at a 'turning point' in their evolution.

2.3. Criticisms of Business Schools

Canals (2011) in a thought-provoking essay focuses on the issue of the espoused purpose of the business school. He identifies a series of crises:

- The *financial and corporate crisis* (e.g. business schools' role in the financial crisis and the ethical and moral crisis associated with corporate scandals such as Enron)
- The need to take *globalisation* and *global talent development* seriously
- The *governance crisis* (the relationship between the business school and the university and the dean's role with respect to faculty)
- The *financial deficit* (the need to examine the sustainability of business schools' business models and funding sources)

- The *relevance deficit* (the perception of the increasing irrelevance of business research)
- Finally, but most importantly, the *humanistic deficit* (the human dimension of fairness in society, the search for stakeholder capitalism, and the examination of the firm and the senior manager's role in society).

Further, the concerns of other eloquent and informed critics must also be recognised. For example:

- Jeff Pfeffer and Christina Fong (2002) at Stanford have suggested that business schools are too market driven and that management research has fallen short of good scientific traditions.
- Henry Mintzberg (2009) has argued that management is an art, not a science, and that the emphasis on analytical methodology and science in business schools is misplaced. He maintains that the traditional MBA curriculum is too narrow and specialised and ignores the development of leadership and management skills.
- The late Sumantra Ghoshal (2005) pointed out the moral decline of business and argued that business schools had been guilty of propagating and teaching 'amoral' theories that destroyed sound management practices.
- Recently, Edwin Locke and J C Spender (2011) amplified Ghoshal's arguments and showed how the business school focus on numbers, mathematical modelling and theories, and specifically those based on financial economics, can lead to rational choices that ignore important issues of culture, managerial behaviour and ethics. They conclude that market capitalism has evolved into 'casino capitalism', largely absent of a moral and ethical compass, in which the lack of financial morality and ethical leadership partially fuelled the global economic crisis of 2008.

Indeed, business schools have been blamed not only for their influence on the global financial crisis but also for ethical business failures such as Enron and WorldCom in the United States and Parmalat in Europe.

Khurana (2007) has observed that a manager's role has shifted from one dedicated to 'higher aims' as professional stewards of a firm's resources to that of 'hired hands' operating only on the basis of contractual relationships. A key consequence of this demoralisation and de-professionalisation of managers is that the self-interest of relevant parties has replaced a proper ethical and moral scope and that the principle of trust that was central to the operation of market capitalism has been abandoned. Clearly, the ethical tradition in business life is in danger of erosion by the institutionalisation of management education and business schools in their current form.

Other critics, including Chris Grey (2005) of Warwick Business School, have argued that business schools have become 'finishing schools' for elites to prepare for positions in finance and consulting without asking them to confront or even examine the ethical and moral challenges of leadership and reflect on their own broader role in society.

2.4. Are There Persistent Problems in Management Education?

It is, therefore, urgent that management educators engage in a period of sustained reflection about the purpose of management education. The important issues they need to consider include the following:

- What is business for?
- What are business schools for?
- Who are the key stakeholders in management education?
- Should the curriculum of management education emphasise breadth and a holistic perspective encompassing disciplines, theories, models, cultures, ethics, social science, history, philosophy and so on and embracing traditions of both analysis and synthesis?

An emerging and important school of thought nurtured by EFMD and promoted by agencies such as EABIS, GLRI, PRME, UN Global Compact and the 50/20 WBSCB group advocates that the business school is a human institution embracing humanistic and societal values and that management education is a creative art and not a deterministic science. It is therefore important to view management education from a wide range of stakeholder perspectives such as society at large, business, government, students and employers. (Yes, current curricula in business schools do pay lip service to these topics though showing more evidence of rhetoric than reality.)

In short, their position is that the sole purpose of firms is not to maximise shareholder wealth. Firms must deploy their power in a socially responsible manner to balance the competing interests of different stakeholders.

However, is this a failure of the capitalist system or is it a result of the financial crisis, bank bailouts and failures, high unemployment, and other economic and social failures in developed countries? Recently, Meltzer (2012) and Zingales (2012) have stoutly defended capitalism as the only philosophy that ensures freedom and economic growth. However, Meltzer argues that failure is an inherent part of capitalism and that scandals such as fraud and corruption are equally present in democracies that are more socialist. Zingales also extols the virtues of capitalism, free markets, deregulation and so on. He believes, however, that business schools are guilty of failing to point out more clearly to their students that an outcome that benefits an individual may have a cost to society.

Chapter 3

The History and Timeline (1971–2012) of EFMD's Growth: EFMD's Role in the Growth of Management Education

3.1. Introduction

Chapter 1 briefly discussed EFMD's history and progress using some of the viewpoints expressed in the *Training the Fire Brigade* (1996) jubilee volume to identify the *raison d'être* and evolution of EFMD as a European management education network.

EFMD came into being in 1971 through the merger of the International University Contact for Management Education (IUC) and the European Association of Management Training Centres (EAMTC). Since then EFMD has stressed its role as Europe's forum for high-quality networking and worldwide co-operation in management education and development. According to Hubert (1996, p. 27) its establishment had three main purposes:

- To serve as a bridge between management practice and management learning
- To dedicate itself to a worldwide exchange of experience and ideas
- To represent management development to third parties.

As noted by Schaik (1996, p. 13), it has clearly sought to link the corporate world and the world of education and hence be a catalyst and a 'broad church' encouraging debate and dialogue between corporations and institutions of management education and learning. Consequently, it has consistently tried to attract a significant proportion of corporate members.

Giovanni Agnelli (1996, p. 117) also emphasises the European identity of EFMD and its preferred European positioning through the 'formation of a distinctly European culture and approach in the field of business and management'.

Hubert (1996, p. 29), however, notes the difficulty over the first 25 years of attracting corporate members to the EFMD network:

> One recurring theme over the years has been the balance in membership between corporate and education/institutional members. All too frequently, EFMD has had the image of an 'association of business schools'.

In this chapter our aim is to identify the timelines and provide insights into the key events in EFMD's evolution, focusing particularly on the last 15 years. We examine the following:

- What have been the key roles, achievements and activities in EFMD's history?
- What were the key challenges and issues in management education discussed in the conclusions to the 1996 volume?
- What have been the key themes and challenges to management education debated in the media since 1996?
- What are the key challenges and themes noted by the interviewees in our research study?
- How many of the challenges identified in the 1996 volume remain unresolved? What challenges and unresolved issues are regarded by key constituencies as critical to the future of management education? (One issue might be, for example, the move to business models that recognise stakeholder management perspectives in framing management education curricula.)

3.2.   The Timelines and Achievements in EFMD's History

The diagram presented in Table 3.1 represents the efforts of Martine Plompen, Matthew Wood and Howard Thomas to identify the key milestones and critical events in EFMD's history.

The history illustrated in Table 3.1 demonstrates clearly the success of EFMD in managing its relationship with educational institutions and in monitoring the quality and content of business school faculty and curricula. From the outset, EFMD has promoted the Annual Deans and Directors' of Business Schools Meeting and the Annual EFMD Conference as networking events for its members. Over time it added the MBA Directors Meeting (1988), the EFMD Guide to MBA Programmes (1990), the Executive Education Network (1992) and the External Relations Network (1994) to reflect the educational diversity of business schools.

Table 3.1: The timeline of EFMD's history: 1972–2012.

	1972	1973	1974	1975	1976	1977	1978	1979	1980
(top)	**Merger of the European Association of Management Training Centres (EAMTC, established 1959) and International University Contact for Management Education (IUC, established 1952)**			**First European Case Development Workshop**		**Honko Report on the Development of Management Teachers and Researchers**		**EC Study: Management Education in the EC Member States**	**Management for the twenty-first century (joint EFMD/AACSB project)**
(bottom)	First EFMD annual conference in Barcelona	First Deans and Directors Meeting	Annual conference in Turin, Italy, exploring the role of management development on changing organisations with Charles Handy as keynote speaker		*Pocock Report on Educational and Training Needs of European Managers* project		*Moucret Report on Management of Management Centres*, proposing an analytical model in terms of • Functions • Operations • Socio-political aspects	The "International Management Development" (IMD) journal becomes a quarterly publication	First Corporate Members Meeting, hosted by Shell

Table 3.1: (Continued)

1981	European societal strategy project focusing on the need to take the changing socio-economic environment into full consideration in developing corporate strategy.
1982	First Public sector Management Development Activity
1983	First Banking Seminar focusing on management development for bankers The Commission of the European Communities commissions EFMD to develop and implement a two-year full-time modular MBA programme in Beijing
1984	China-EEC Management Programme (CEMP) in Beijing is aimed at educating 100 young Chinese managers over a five-year period. Teaching is provided by visiting faculty from Europe recruited by EFMD
1985	Launch of the European Women's Management Development Network
1986	Strategic Audit Unit: Analysis by international teams of peers helps schools to improve quality and strategic capability European Enterprises Employment Project
1987	Launch of the European Business Ethics Network
1988	First MBA Directors Meeting
1989	Contribution to ERT, European Roundtable of industrialists report on HR management First Case Writing Competition
1990	China-Europe Management Institute (CEMI) started to institutionalise the China activities. In addition to the MBA, executive courses are offered and foreign companies start to support the school financially First EFMD guide to MBA programmes

Timeline 1991–2001

1991	New series of practice orientated workshops for corporate members · Euro-Algerian cooperation programme
1992	Executive Education Network · Euro-CIS Program focused on institution building and transfer on knowledge and skills
1993	First EFMD EC Dialogue seminar with European Commission officials on trends in the EC programmes · C.K. Prahalad delivers keynote address at the annual conference focusing on strategies for growth
1994	External Relations Group launched · Joint venture to establish the China-Europe International Business School (CEIBS), Shanghai
1995	Best Practice Projects, an EC supported work on corporate re-engineering and the management of change · Launch of EQUAL, the European Quality Link for Management Education
1996	Euro-Arab Management School · Publication of *Training the Fire Brigade: Preparing for the unimaginable* on the occasion of 25th anniversary
1997	Launch of EQUIS, with 18 pioneer schools · The EFMD Board now has two vice presidents, one from the business school side and one from the corporate side
1998	*European Management Education Report*, providing overview of management education systems in Europe · Move to Rue Gachard offices · Establishment of EQUIS standards and criteria · New advisory service (EQUIP) established
1999	EQUIS accredits first school outside Europe (HEC Montreal) · Most comprehensive Executive Education Directory becomes available · Launch of the Corporate University Learning Group
2000	Launch of the new initiative on first degree programmes · Report on Return-On-Investment Learning Group · New EFMD Director General, Eric Cornuel
2001	Executive education Faculty Development Programme · Start of e-learning expedition project · Corporate Special Interest Groups launched

Timeline 2002–2011

2002	First version of the CLIP quality improvement guidelines and standards · First CLIP pilot self-assessment and pilot review · Co-organisation of Bangkok Global Forum · Launch of Global Responsibility Initiative and Manifesto
2003	First new deans seminar · EFMD organises corporate task force on coaching · Launch of EntreNews, EFMD's Entrepreneurship,
2004	Establishment of GFME — Global Foundation for Management Education · Take off of GRLI, in partnership with UN Global Compact · Formation of CEL Awarding Body
2005	Launch of EPAS, programme accreditation system · Publication of special issue of the *Journal of Management Development* and two EFMD books: *Should Prometheus*
2006	EFMD Advisory Services launched · Organisation of successful first conference in China · Launch of the Best Practice
2007	Launch of IDP — International Deans Programme · Launch of Excellence in practice Awards on partnerships for Learning and Development
2008	Publication of *CLIP Research Report* · Over 700 members in the EFMD network · Largest ever EFMD annual conference
2009	Launch of EU Presidency Steering Committee · Launch of the Business in Society · Opening of the EFMD office in China
2010	First conference in MENA region and first Africa conference · Corporate Workplace Learning Special Interest Groups · Launch of Research
2011	EFMD Asia established · Launch of DAF — Deans Across Frontiers

Table 3.1: (Continued)

New EFMD website	Innovation and Small Business Network newsletter	Launch of Outstanding Doctoral Awards, in partnership with Emerald group Publishing	be Bound? and Innovative Corporate Learning	Sharing CLIP workshops	EQUIS 10th anniversary	Publication of the CLIP Research Report	Leadership programme with EURAM Round Table Initiative on the future of management education
Launch of Global Marketing Game	First joint conference with the Canadian Federation of Business School Deans	10th anniversary of CEIBS, the joint venture between EFMD and Jiaotong University	Launch of the new EFMD website at EFMD.org and members area		Publication of EFMD Public Sector Case Book	The first joint GMAC/EFMD Corporate Recruiters Survey	First MSc programme directors conference
Launch of EFMD electronic newsletter		Launch of corporate SPIGS — Special Interest Group Series			Launch of new EFMD magazine Global Focus		Global Focus magazine now available in Chinese
					Record number of participants in 2007 EFMD conferences: 1200		
					EQUIS accredits its 100th school		
					Search tool for executive education of EFMD website		
					CLIP process and criteria revised		
					Launch of the IDP — International Deans Programme, in partnership with ABS		
					Launch of the EFMD Excellence in Practice Awards		
					Development of the PRME initiative (Principles for Responsible Management education)		

1st Higher Education Research Conference

2012

Round Table Initiative on the Future of Management Education

Source: Plompen, Wood (EFMD) and HThomas.

More recently it has launched a number of global initiatives such as the Global Leadership Responsibility Initiative (GLRI) and, in association with AACSB International, the Global Foundation for Management Education (GFME), which focus on leadership challenges both for society as a whole and for different regions and cultures.

Throughout, EFMD has also been concerned with the quality and relevance of management research and the associated capability of management faculty to perform management teaching and research. Following the *Honko Report* (EFMD Reports, 1977), which focused on the supply and demand of and for faculty, EFMD built an alliance with the European Institute of Advanced Studies in Management (EIASM) — originally funded by the Ford Foundation — to enhance research quality and to professionalise the disciplines of management research. Together they subsidised the development (by the early 1990s) of the European Marketing Academy, the European Finance Association, the European International Business Association, the European Accounting Association, the European Business Ethics Network and the European Foundation for Entrepreneurship Research.

All of these have prospered and contributed to enhancing the quality of European management research. EFMD also set up its own research committee in 2010, which held the first Conference on the Future of Management Education in 2012 in Zurich, Switzerland.

EFMD has had relatively less success in building its corporate membership despite promoting a wide range of corporate activities (corporate membership reached a peak proportion of 40% of all members in the mid-1980s). For example, it launched the first Corporate Members Meeting in 1980 following reports such as the 1976 *Pocock Report on the Educational and Training Needs of European Managers* and the 1978 *Moucret Report on the Management of Management Centres.*

Subsequent activities in 1982 in public sector management, the European enterprises employment project in 1986 and the Best Practice Project (1995) further reinforced EFMD's desire for a strong corporate focus. In turn, this has led to the LINK programme (2001), supporting management education professionals, the formation of corporate special interest groups (2001) and the CLIP quality improvement standards and subsequent best practice workshops for executive education (from 2002–2006). In addition, in 2008 EFMD joined with the Graduate Management Admissions Council (GMAC) to produce a corporate recruiters survey.

Throughout its existence, EFMD has insisted that its governance, and particularly its Board, should have a balance between corporate and business education members. In 1997 the Board, for the first time, instituted the practice of having two vice-presidents, one from the business school side and one from the corporate side, an innovation that has continued to the present day.

One area of real strength for EFMD has been its internationalism, gained through its various partnerships with the European Union and the European Commission, starting with the China Project in 1983/84. The Commission first asked EFMD to develop and implement a two-year full-time modular MBA programme in Beijing in 1983. The China-EEC Management Development Programme (CEMP) in Beijing, aimed at educating 100 young Chinese managers over a five-year period, followed this in 1984. By 1990 the China-Europe Management Institute (CEMI) had been started in order to institutionalise the MBA and executive education activities in China. This led subsequently to a joint-venture project with the European Union to form the China Europe International Business School (CEIBS) in Shanghai in 1994. CEIBS is now a highly successful and strongly ranked global business school.

EFMD has also collaborated with the European Union on a wide range of other overseas projects such as the Euro-India and the Euro-Algeria Co-operation programmes in 1991, the Euro-CIS (Commonwealth of Independent States) programme on institution building in 1992, the launch of CEEMAN (the Central and Eastern Europe Management Development Association in 1993) and the Euro-Arab Management School in 1996.

All of these international projects have gradually built a strong global footprint for EFMD and created its deserved reputation as the most internationally oriented of the professional/trade management education organisations. This resulted in the opening of an EFMD office in China in 2009 and the first EFMD Conferences in both the Middle East and Africa in 2010.

In its history, EFMD has also wrestled with the issue of quality standards and accreditation standards for management education. It started somewhat tentatively in 1986 with the formation of the Strategic Audit Unit, which sought to help schools to improve their quality and competence on a consulting basis through expert peer team visits and analyses. In 1995 the EQUAL network initiative (an alliance with organisations such as ABS, AMBA and AACSB) was formed to specify international quality assurance standards and approaches. It was not long after this that the EFMD Board decided in 1997 to launch its own European accreditation system (EQUIS), paralleling AACSB's more North American focused programme, with a group of 18 pioneer schools. In 1999 it accredited its first school outside Europe (HEC Montreal in Canada) and now has accredited around 150 schools worldwide.

In 2004 it augmented EQUIS with EPAS, a programme (not an institutional) accreditation scheme, and has recently launched Dean Across Frontiers (DAF) to improve quality standards in less developed areas of the world. It has also promoted accreditation for management development and executive education programmes through the CLIP scheme (2002–2006).

EFMD has adopted a broad focus on environmental issues, sustainability, the social and societal dimension of management and public-sector management. This reflects European views of capitalism, which embrace social democratic models rather than the somewhat more focused models of free-market capitalism common in North America. For example, EFMD has sponsored the development of the Global Leadership Responsibility Initiative (GLRI) from 2004 together with the UN Global Compact, which adopts a set of principles for responsible management education. More recently (2012), EFMD has produced a draft manifesto for management education that advocates a clear stakeholder perspective on management education.

3.3. What Were the Challenges for Management Education Identified in the 1996 Volume? What Roles Were Suggested for EFMD's Future?

By 1996 — the 25th anniversary of EFMD — it had clearly fulfilled a number of its goals. It had established a distinctive European network with a global footprint encompassing a range of initiatives in the Middle East, India, China, and Central and Eastern Europe. This international diversity, both regionally and culturally, has been reinforced by its relentless desire to embrace the constant challenge of attracting corporate and public-sector managers as members alongside deans and leaders of educational institutions.

Even so, the contributors to the 1996 volume drew out a number of key challenges facing EFMD at that time. They include the following, with relevant quotes from 1996.

3.3.1. Embracing the Ideas and Principles of a Liberal Education

In his 1996 essay, Charles Handy reflected that:

> It is odd, to say the least, that the education of our managers has so little in it about personality theory, what makes people what they are; or about learning theory, how people grow and develop and change; or political theory, how people seek power, resist power and organise themselves; or moral philosophy, how they decide between right and wrong.
>
> It is odd, too, that so little attention is paid, during this education, to history where all these aspects of people are laid

out before us, and where the influences which work on them can be seen in the clearer beam of hindsight. History never repeats itself, but it does help one to learn to disentangle the forces which shape events, a skill essential to management and leadership.

All of this is even odder when one considers that our business schools are, for the most part, set in the context of a University or Institute where Psychology, Politics, Philosophy and History are almost certainly part of the established faculty. It was a mistake, I now believe, to have established our business schools as a race apart from so much else in education. (Handy, 1996, p. 11)

Handy's critique is an emphatic plea for grounding management education in the tradition of a liberal education, with less time spent on the more formulaic, mechanical and specialisation aspects of the management task. He views (1996, p. 208) some management schools as instrumental and unexciting. He believes that they should make learning fun, a process of discovering new worlds rather than an unexciting exploration of the mechanics of the management process.

3.3.2.   A New Era of Innovation and Change

The theme of change, discovery and exploration is endorsed by Professor Pedro Nueno (1996, p. 55), who stresses that management education is at a point of inflexion and entering a new era of innovation, transformation and global growth in which we should discover new ways of doing things rather than looking for ways to achieve greater efficiency. He believes that management education should focus on some of the critical areas essential to future growth, namely, entrepreneurship, innovation, institutional co-operation, and growth achieved through free trade and globalisation.

3.3.3.   Competition, the Pace of Change and Increasing Stakeholder Pressure

George Bain (1996, p. 89) similarly focuses on strategic change and identifies three main trends in the business environment: the increasing scope and intensity of global competition; the increasing pace of change (through technology and global competition); and the increasing stakeholder pressure on organisations (to address performance standards beyond economic criteria to embrace social, environmental and ethical aspects). Each of these has implications for strategy and operations.

Companies will need to compete on clearly understood strategic capabilities, innovatory ideas and core competences in the context of the need for rapid and flexible strategic change. He predicts that corporate structures will become leaner with less command and control processes and much flatter organisational processes. This has clear implications for management education and for training managers in the core skills and capabilities necessary for managing change.

There will be a need for continuous learning as the shelf life of an MBA will shorten considerably. Managerial careers will be less predictable and managers will become more mobile. There will be a focus in management education, particularly executive education, on lifelong learning and issues associated with topics such as leadership, skills in problem identification and corporate vision and abilities in contextual, cultural, global and emotional intelligence.

3.3.4. The Challenge of Globalisation and the Importance of European Models of Management Education

Claude Rameau (1996, p. 57) reinforces the global aspect of change and the advantages of European management education:

> Europe and European management should be an inspiration for the rest of the world. It is more diverse, it is richer, it now has more experience than the rest of the world can offer, including the United States. The business schools should take advantage of that and EFMD should take the leading role in offering all of it to the world.

Giovanni Agnelli (1996, p. 117), the then chairman of Italy's FIAT group, also believes that it is important to address 'the formation of a distinctly European culture and approach in the field of business and management'.

3.3.5. Recognising the Realities of Strategic Growth and Change

The late C.K. Prahalad (1996, p. 105) and Gary Hamel (1996, p. 113) are well-respected writers in the strategy field and, arguably, the pioneers of the concept of leveraging strategic core competences in organisational contexts. In 1996 they commented on the need for strategic change in Europe and both focused on the need for a strategic growth agenda for Europe and for clear changes in management education.

Dramatic growth, in the context of developing new industries in Europe, requires 'a radical rethinking of current management paradigms' (Prahalad, 1996, p. 109). Hamel (1996, p. 113) argues that the 'race to the future, to create the new (emerging) industries ... [means] we are standing on the verge of a new industrial revolution dealing with genetics, materials, and, more than anything else, information'. He goes on: 'as we look to the future, we have to consider a totally new way of looking at competition'.

Both Hamel and Prahalad strongly believe that the curricula in management education have become trapped in somewhat obsolete textbooks and in stories of past corporate experiences (i.e. case studies). New management theories, business models and paradigms are needed in the new growth environment.

Hamel comments: 'What we continue to teach in the business schools is a little bit like being a mapmaker in an earthquake zone. Never before has the gap between our tools and the reality of emerging industry been larger' (Hamel, 1996, p. 113).

He also criticises business schools for their alleged corporate blindness: 'For years most business schools assumed their product was the MBA. It's not; it's competitiveness. The only contribution business schools can make to society is to improve competitiveness and, therefore, the potential for wealth creation. How many business schools look at what they do through the lines of: "What is the contribution we made last year to competitiveness?"'

3.3.6.   Adapting Curricula to the Realities of Growth and Societal/Stakeholder Perspectives

Peter Lorange (1996, pp. 141, 142), the then president of IMD and now of the Lorange Institute of Business in Zurich, Switzerland, also challenges the role of business schools in the future. He believes that business schools will still exist in the next 25 years (i.e. up to 2021) but that their teaching portfolios and foci will have to change. While he notes that the MBA will still be around, it will be important for the student to gain the qualification from a high-quality, high-reputation school — that will matter more than the qualification itself. More than anything else he implores business schools (and EFMD) to try new ideas and be inquisitive about them:

> We should help regions, countries, organisations to develop. We should look at curious phenomena and situations and ask more about them. Why for example, should Manila in the

Philippines be cited as having the best managed 'company' in South East Asia for several years running (San Miguel) despite the other Asian 'Tigers'. What can we learn from this?

His overall comment is that new business school models are needed. Business schools, for example, should be more open and inquisitive about problems in society and seek to improve human and moral values in society.

3.3.7. The Possibility That Inertia and Complacency May Create Failure for Business Schools

Michael Osbaldeston (1996, pp. 215, 216) also focuses on themes addressed by Hamel, Prahalad and Lorange. He asks: 'Why might business schools not be as successful as they might wish to be in the future?' He suggests that inertia to change may be a real issue: 'It could be a combination of the difficulty of escaping from your past, with an inability to create the future, or contentment with a track record of past and current performance'.

Beyond inertia, complacency with the *status quo* can also be a pressing issue, with faculty sometimes being the impediments to change. 'Our core competence is invested in the faculty; so if we recruit the right people, then surely the right people will deliver the right business school of the future'.

Sadly, faculty often hold strong views and well-formed recipes about good education and research. They often do not see the need to reinvent the future.

3.4. What Have Been the Key Challenges and Themes About Management Education in the Media?

3.4.1. Media Highlights of Management Education and Business Schools (1990s–Present)

Figure 3.1 provides a schematic diagram showing the major events in the economic and business school environment mapped against the major themes and critiques of business schools in the popular media.

Over the past two decades business schools and management education have been in the media spotlight over a range of issues, with the most important issues recurring and brought up consistently throughout the years. The value and relevancy of an MBA appears to be a key issue that is usually raised, albeit questioned by different stakeholders in different contexts.

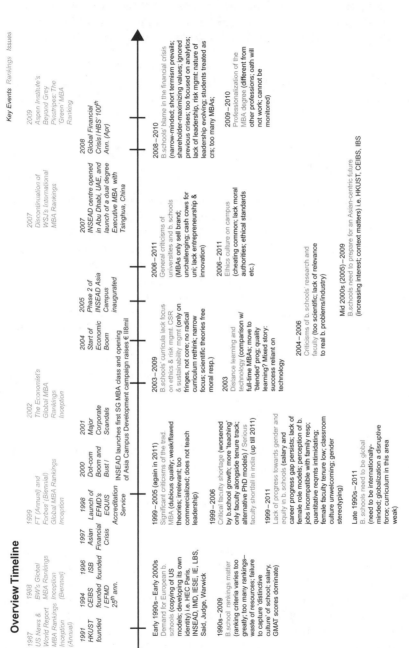

Figure 3.1: Media highlights of management education and business schools, 1990s–Present.

In the early 1990s, the focus seems to be on business school's ability to meet the specialised needs of businesses. Critics questioned the conventional MBA and its usefulness to businesses, with more emphasis on schools in the United States than in the United Kingdom or any other regions. The criticism then shifted its focus to whether the inadequate nature and irrelevancy of management research is the fundamental problem for business schools' curricula weaknesses.

Media discussion of business schools and management education appears closely related to economic performance. The dotcom boom and bust years of the late 1990s and early 2000s illustrated a trend towards increased commercialisation of business schools. Much attention was paid, for example, to how business schools could manage increased student enrolments while simultaneously facing a shortage of top educators. During the 2004 economic boom, when demand for MBA students was also strong, schools were again questioned over their academic credibility. This time it was over whether they were training students correctly given such major corporate scandals as Enron and WorldCom.

In recent years, the 2008 recession generated more questioning of business schools' role in the recession and society and the continued absence of much about ethics and risk management in their curricula. This has led to a lot of attention focused on business schools' actions in improving their current structures and the urgent need to evolve and change the business school model, an issue that smoothly transitions into concern of how schools can incorporate the issue of globalisation when restructuring their curricula.

The issue of incorporating sustainability and the notion of the 'triple bottom line' (people, planet, profit) into the business curriculum has been raised since the early days of this century and is still relevant in current discussions.

The emerging trend appears to be a wider focus on stakeholder management and an exploration of newer forms of learning, including action learning and technology enhanced learning.

Other issues such as gender equity in MBA enrolments, popularisation of MBA media rankings and professionalisation of management were raised as well but have not received so much attention in the last two decades.

3.4.2. Media Highlights on Management Education and Business Schools (1990–2011): Overview of the Main Themes

We have identified 15 main media themes ranging from the popularity of the MBA in business to business school rankings. We have attached an illustrative quote to each theme.

They broadly reflect the continued questioning of the MBA and the relevance to business of management education in general. Relevance is also linked to economic performance and the role management education may have played in various ethical and global financial crises. This leads to a wider questioning of the role of business and management education in society with stronger stakeholder perspectives becoming increasingly evident.

1. Popularity of Business Schools
   a. Change in attitude in the United Kingdom towards B-schools
- 'There is a copying of America. People see the MBA as a way to accelerate their careers'. (Leo Murray, former dean of the Cranfield School of Management, UK)

   b. Some European companies are still not receptive towards MBAs
- *Indeed, some European companies shun holders of MBAs, calling them* prima donnas *who do not deserve the salaries they clamour for.* (Steven Greenhouse, 'In Europe, a boom in MBAs', New York Times, 29 May 1991)

   c. UK business schools must improve their management education performance
- *Companies in general have been far more willing to tackle new methods of learning than universities. Even young business school faculty members are adopting conventional approaches to teaching.* (*CEML: Characteristics of the Management Population in the UK: Overview Report;* Linda Anderson, *'Leadership training needs to improve', Financial Times*, 12 May 2002)

   d. European business schools are developing their own identity
- *At first many of the European schools copied the American model. Now they are slowly developing their own identities, relying more on European case studies and building a more European faculty. They also have become far more international than the American schools.* (Pedro Nueno) (Steven Greenhouse, 'In Europe, a boom in MBAs', *New York Times*, 29 May 1991)

2. Evolution of the Traditional MBA
   a. Curriculum has to change to meet student needs
- *The curriculum has changed to meet the new needs of students. Electives like agribusiness and public administration that had been popular now find less favour than courses with titles like management technology, managing for quality, and starting and managing a small business.* (Elizabeth M. Fowler, 'Careers; Management School Shifts with Times', *New York Times*, 30 Jan 1990)

b. Executive education programmes preferred to traditional MBA
   - *Many prefer to fill their needs by sending managers already on staff to one of the thousands of 'executive education' programs that have sprung up.* ('B-schools under fire', 'The Chief Executive', CE Roundtable Panel Discussion, April 1993)
c. Variations on the traditional MBA
   - *Another important factor to consider: cost — the shorter the course, the more you can charge per hour (greater marginal revenue for schools). Students are willing to pay more for a shorter time. (Landis Gabel, former dean of INSEAD)* ('Definitely shorter, maybe sweeter too', *The Economist*, 4 March 2003)
d. Commercialisation of B-schools
   - *Indeed, some of the myriad MBA programs are* 'of dubious quality'. (John Quelch, former dean of London Business School) (Alan Cowell, 'International Business; British MBA courses shake up old school'. *New York Times*, November 1999)
e. Demand for MBA has levelled off
   - *The important point, however, is that the growth of students seeking MBA degrees has levelled off, and as a result we are behaving like any other industry where growth has slowed: we are competing intensely.* (Colin Blaydon, dean of Amos Tuck Graduate School of Business at Dartmouth College) (Eric N Berg, 'Talking business; with Blaydon of Amos Tuck; easing the cost of MBA degree', *New York Times*, 20 March 1990)

3. The Value of an MBA
a. Curriculum should be more closely aligned to the needs of business
   - *While acknowledging the need for substantial change, business school deans say the disparities between the supply and demand for their product are also partly the fault of CEOs, who often send mixed signals to campuses; CEOs continue to hire MBAs in substantial numbers despite their complaints.* ('B-schools under fire', 'The Chief Executive', CE Roundtable Panel Discussion, April 1993)
b. Graduates criticised for adopting an analytical and quantitative approach to business issues when companies needed managers with more diffuse soft skills such as leadership
   - *B-schools tend to concentrate on 'elegant, abstract models' that seek to unify world economic systems rather than help students understand 'the messy, concrete reality of international business'.* (Elizabeth M. Fowler, 'Careers; Rethinking business education', *New York Times*, 19 Jun 1990)

    c. B-school curriculum is not rigorous enough
- *Some professors complained that setting up a business school would be crass and commercial and that the MBA degree would be less academically rigorous than Oxford's other graduate degrees.* (Steven Greenhouse, 'In Europe, a boom in MBAs', *New York Times*, 29 May 1991)

    d. A business school's value is mostly derived from its reputation, a carefully cultivated brand and networking, with other minor factors at play such as timing.
- *Most HBS students acknowledge that much of the Harvard MBA's value is derived from outside the classroom: the access to rich networks at social functions, the brand name degree-essentially, the promise of a better and brighter future.* (Tara W. Merrigan, 'A brand name MBA', *The Harvard Crimson*, 27 May 2010)

    e. The MBA is useful, a versatile and broad degree that is applicable to any field
- *The MBA is the most versatile degree out there — most of the others are very field specific, but you can apply an MBA to any field.* (Rachel Edgington, research director, GMAC) (Abby Ellin, 'Was earning that MBA worth it?', *New York Times*, 11 Jun 2006)

    f. Schools need to be more innovative
- *The region may be blessed with high-quality scientific research, but too much of it fails to make it to the realms of innovation — There is a need to learn to bring the science and business communities together efficiently.* (Alfons Sauquet, dean of ESADE Business School, 'Only connect', *The Economist*, 9 Jun 2010)

4. B-Schools' Research and Faculty
    a. Research is not helpful to business, has little to do with real business problems and does not translate into practical relevant skills for students
- *B-schools' specialty — research-seems to be of little value.* ('B-schools under fire', 'The Chief Executive', CE Roundtable Panel Discussion, April 1993)

    b. Faculty members lack business experience
- *Business schools' research agendas must become primarily driven by real-life management problems. But in order for this change to happen, problem-driven research must become recognised and honoured as a great way to advance, not jeopardise, an academic career.* (Richard Schmalensee, 'Where's the "B" in B-schools?', *Business Week*, 27 November 2006)

5. Faculty Shortage

a. A rising number of business schools and other factors such as retiring baby boomers, expensive doctoral programmes facing budget cuts, falling interest in becoming business B-school academics are causing a shortage of (good) faculty

- *Besides the growing number of B-schools in the US, there has been an explosion of such schools in other countries that are seeking American-trained faculty with doctoral degrees.* (Lisa Cornwell, 'Business schools face faculty shortage', *Boston Globe*, 20 February 2006)

b. Implications of a faculty shortage on B-schools

- *Business education experts say a continuing shortage of doctoral faculty in business will hurt the quality of research and teaching and leave future business executives less prepared for leadership roles in a global economy.* (Lisa Cornwell, 'Business schools face faculty shortage', *Boston Globe*, 20 February 2006)

c. It is increasingly difficult to lure top educators to B-schools; salaries and benefits have been rising accordingly

- *Salaries and benefits are rising accordingly. It is particularly hard to lure the brightest stars in subjects like finance, accounting, marketing, strategy.* (Robert Hansen, former dean of Tuck School of Business) ('The hunt for good professors', *The Economist*, 8 May 2003)

d. B-schools step up efforts in tackling faculty shortage

- *Universities have compensated for the PhD shortage by having their PhDs delay retirement, by recruiting mid-career business executives and by emphasising teaching instead of research.* ('A few good professors: U.S. business schools suffer a dearth of doctorates', *Knowledge@W.P. Carey*, 6 Jun 2007)

6. B-Schools Need to Prepare for Asia-Centric Future

a. There is new demand for more MBAs and executive MBAs within Japan and China

- *As Japan emerges from a long recession, some aspiring managers are pursuing an MBA to improve their chances in the reviving job-market [while] Japanese companies seeking to expand abroad are sending employees on MBA programmes at American business schools.* ('The degreed salaryman', *The Economist*, 19 Jan 2005)

b. China and India's top B-schools are capable of producing future global leaders

- *Are the leading B-schools in China and India up to the task, or will the grooming of tomorrow's global leaders be done primarily at institutions such as Harvard, Stanford, and INSEAD? Notwithstanding the apparent dominance of western — especially American — business schools, the odds favour the top schools from within China and India. Student quality at the top Indian and Chinese schools is superb and getting better. Domestic salaries received by graduates of the top MBA programmes in both China and India are rising and becoming competitive with their counterparts in the West. ... Attractive salaries and abundant job prospects would suggest that the indigenous MBA programmes will become even more attractive to the top domestic applicants in the coming years.* (Anil K. Gupta and Haiyan Wang, 'The odds favour business schools in China and India', *Business Week*, 8 May 2009)

7. Corporate Social Responsibility and Sustainability

a. B-schools are stepping up to make CSR a core part of their curriculum
   - *Slowly but surely, more business schools are moving from bolt-on sustainability initiatives to much more building-in to research, teaching and practice — and to the schools' own roles as employers and customers.* (David Grayson, 'What business schools can do to encourage sustainability', *Guardian*, 11 March 2011)

b. Students are a huge factor in B-schools' increased efforts to incorporate the concept of sustainability in their curriculum
   - *Today's students are already putting pressure on schools to promote sustainability through organisations such as Net Impact, the global movement for MBAs, and other students interested in the responsibilities of business and how to make a difference.* (David Grayson, 'What business schools can do to encourage sustainability' *Guardian*, 11 March 2011)

c. Boutique B-schools that place high emphasis on sustainability are limited in scope
   - *Those in the field say that the focus of these M.B.A. programs (smaller schools that place high emphasis on sustainability in their curriculum) is the wave of the future, although their narrow scope is not without its limitations.* (Abby Ellin, 'MBAs with three bottom lines: People, Planet and Profit', *New York Times*, 8 January 2006)

d. B-schools and relevant bodies need to start acknowledging the importance of CSR and sustainability
   - *A recent joint survey by the UN and the consultancy Accenture [found that] 72% of chief executive officers believe education must be key in ensuring the acceptance of the need for a sustainable approach to business doesn't die out but instead becomes the accepted norm of the future.* (Giselle Weybrecht, 'How to make business schools teach green', *Forbes*, 16 July 2010)

8. Business Students Cheat and Lack Integrity

a. Cheating is prevalent despite efforts to create a culture of ethics

- *Despite recent efforts to create a culture of ethics on business school campuses, cheating remains all too common. A group of professors finds that 56% of business-school students admitted to cheating one or more times in the past academic year.* ('Lacking integrity', *The Economist*, 25 September 2006)

b. B-school deans have huge responsibility

- *A growing perception [is that] many deans of business schools are ineffective because many appeared to lack any moral authority as leaders. [Few] treat the problem of cheating as a serious issue and look away when confronted with ethical issues, students will do the same.* (Michael Friedlander, 'Ethics, student cheating and the business school deans: How looking away is not a badge of honor', 12 February 2011)

9. Ethics and Risk Management

a. Ethics needs to be integrated into all MBA coursework

- *Schools should ratchet up the study of business ethics — not just the consequences of scandals but also positive examples and everyday ethical choices inherent in the lives of managers. Existing research on corporate ethics pales in comparison with other subjects.* (Jennifer Merritt, 'Ethics is also B-school business', *Business Week*, 17 January 2003)

b. Complex mathematical models need to be reviewed for risk management

- *Other experts think B-schools should go even further by not only increasing the no. of courses they offer, but also revising their syllabi, which currently focus heavily on mathematical modeling.* (Laura Fitzpatrick, 'Will business schools learn from Wall Street's crisis?', *Time*, 21 September 2008)

c. B-schools are not entirely to blame for corporate scandals

- *The clutch[s] of top executives currently on trial for corporate corruption are notable for their lack of B-school qualifications.* ('Bad for business?' *The Economist*, 17 February 2005)

10. Professionalisation of MBA Degrees

a. MBA degrees should be professionalised

- *Advocates say MBA should include many of the same elements that degrees in law and medicine incorporate — such as making the degree mandatory for certain positions, competency testing similar to the bar exam for lawyers, and most important a sense of responsibility*

to society. (Francesca Di Meglio, 'MBAs: Public enemy no. 1?' *Business Week*, 20 May 2009)
b. Professionalisation of MBA degrees is hardly a panacea
   - *No one would argue that lawyers, doctors and accountants are immune from wrongdoing or poor judgement, and they have long been taking certification exams and promising to act ethically.* (Kelley Holland, 'Is it time to retrain B-schools?' *New York Times*, 15 March 2009)

11. Who's to Blame?/Role of the B-Schools

a. Schools focus too much on maximising shareholder value
   - *Business school teaching that is based on shareholder value maximisation can easily turn it into an ideology where truth becomes a victim of good intentions. One such simplification [of complex business issues] that has dominated most MBA teaching is the assumption that shareholder value is something that is achievable and can solve the problems of economic efficiency, prosperity and growth all at once.* (Ismail Erturk, 'Business schools need to go back to business school', *Top MBA*, 1 September 2009)
b. Business media has a role to play as well; influencing B-schools in being more concerned about media rankings than imparting good decision-making skills
   - *While the shareholder maximisation model gathered steam, business schools began fighting for top spots in media rankings. Some educators are asking business media to take a look in the mirror before pointing the finger at B-schools alone for today's problems ... business school rankings have helped to turn students into consumers and business schools into businesses.* (Francesca Di Meglio, 'MBAs: Public enemy no. 1?' *Business Week*, 20 May 2009)
c. B-schools are in the position to lead the world economy out of recession
   - *Will tomorrow's leaders be able to reverse the distrust born from the recent financial collapse? The continued popularity of the MBA degree suggests that many employers, business schools and students are betting yes.* (Dan Beaudry, 'Responsible leadership: The truth about risk', *Top MBA*, 4 October 2010)

12. Globalisation

a. Specialised knowledge is no longer sufficient; it's important to have an integrated worldview
   - *What is needed in this increasingly competitive, global economy is not just specialised know-how but its opposite: an integrated world view.* ('The bigger picture', *The Economist*, 8 May 2003)

b. Challenges in embracing the changes to making business education truly international

- *Despite lamenting the pace of change, the growth and diversity of options available to business school students is to be praised, suggesting that the sector is on the verge of a new era in which national boundaries cease to matter.* (Sarah Cunnane, 'Bridge the global gap, business schools urged', *Times Higher Education*, 17 February 2011)

13. Lack of Progress Towards Gender and Equity in B-Schools

a. Slow progress in gender and equity (faculty and students)

- *Women have made great strides in business but the glass ceiling is far from completely shattered. Business schools are lagging behind many corporations in providing a supportive environment for women.* (Francesca Di Meglio, 'Breaking B-schools' gender barrier', *Business Week*, 1 December 2004)

b. The business school curriculum/culture is not conducive or favourable towards women

- *MBA recruiters need to press schools to catch up with corporations, which often are more progressive [than business schools] in pursuing gender-based programmes and creating more inclusive environments.* (Francesca Di Meglio, 'Breaking B-schools' gender barrier', *Business Week*, 1 December 2004)

c. Corporations are making efforts to empower women through business education

- *Goldman Sachs set aside $100 million over five years to bring business education to 10,000 qualified women business owners in developing countries, a commitment that remains unchanged despite banking industry turmoil.* (Elizabeth Olson, 'Businesses see opportunity in empowering women', *New York Times*, 25 December 2008)

14. Distance-Learning and Technology

a. Distance-learning could be key

- *One of the most important benefits is that rather than squirreling themselves away in academic isolation, distance-learning students can apply what they learn on their programmes the very next morning in the workplace, making it the most practical way to study.* ('Why distance-learning MBAs matter', *The Economist*, 14 February 2010)

b. Does distance-learning represent quality learning?

- *Academics stress that because distance-learning students must pass the same assessment criteria and sit for the same exams as their on-campus peers, they enjoy the same recognition from their institution.* ('Why distance-learning MBAs matter', *The Economist*, 14 February 2010)

15. MBA Media Rankings
   a. B-schools pay more attention to rankings (than other professional schools)
      - *An attempt by Harvard and Wharton to lead a boycott of the rankings in 2005 did not, in the end, muster much support. Most schools now accept — albeit sometimes grudgingly — that they have been broadly beneficial. And the marketing departments can't get enough. After all, the more rankings there are, the more chance there is to be number one at something.* ('Ups and downs', *The Economist*, 15 October 2009)
   b. Rankings discrepancy and inconsistency
      - *AACSB [claims] compilers are using inconsistent data and subjective opinions. It argues that the rankers put too much emphasis on short-term performance and often ignore the part-time pro-grammes that serve approximately 80% of America's MBA students.* ('Rank Disagreement', *The Economist*, 25 October 2005)

3.5. What Are the Ongoing Challenges and Themes Identified by Our Research Interviewees?

Respondents were asked what they considered the biggest ongoing challenges confronting management education. Their responses fall into three broad categories: the *role* — and *perception* — of management education in society; and the *external* and *internal* conditions confronting the management education industry.

Figure 3.2 gives a schematic mapping of the key challenges and themes. The elements in the diagram are explained, with illustrations from the respondents, in this section: the role, and perception, of management education in society and external/internal conditions affecting the management education industry.

3.5.1. Role, and Perception, of Management Education in Society

Many respondents question whether management education, and indeed business schools, has yet established a clear identity and positioning for developing management education in society. Questions recur about whether management education is relevant, either to business or to academia, and whether curricula are broad enough to develop skills such as leadership,

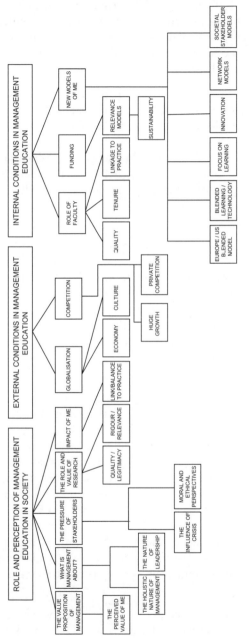

Figure 3.2: Ongoing challenges in management education.

managerial styles, problem identification and critical thinking. In essence, they question the 50–100 year legacy of formal management education.

There is, above all, a perception problem with management education. Put simply, management education is not seen as worth the effort. For example, one UK respondent questioned the value proposition of management education in the following terms:

> I think that there's a perception problem, and I think that is something we see so strongly here in the UK is that people do not value it. I think that it's a real, real problem.

3.5.1.1. The Perceived Value of Management Education/Programme Homogeneity Others question the generic and rather homogeneous orientation of management education and reinforce issues of value and programme homogeneity.

> I asked the MBA directors of the top 100 schools on the *FT* list how much of the content in their MBA is from their own faculty and how much is just generic. And the response was that 90% of it was generic. So you are using the same Kotler marketing book, the same Brealey/Myers finance books, the same Harvard cases and every now and then the instructor can pepper his or her class with either war stories or a particular research project they are working on. But there isn't massive differentiation.

Says another:

> I frankly think that telling the next generation and future generations of students how Dell got it right, how Canon got it right and how Apple is just wonderful with the iPhone and iPad is pretty trivial. And my view then is that unless the schools start addressing what I would count as pressing managerial issues, global issues and so on then the disconnect with society grows larger.

3.5.1.2. What is Management About? There are a range of concerns about the sterility and obsolescence of current curricula and the lack of understanding of the management process. One respondent sees us 'stuck in the past'.

> I also see another challenge. There are many new realities that may make management education as we know it a bit obsolete. Essentially, many of the traditional programmes, the MBA, even the Advanced Management Programme, actually

assume a state of the world as it was, let's say, 30, 40 or 50 years ago.

While another sees us as slow to adapt to new realities of globalisation.

Speaking globally, the recurrent challenge … is that we don't know what a practising manager needs to do and succeed. I think that we'll always have a challenge regarding whether what we do is fit for purpose.

Yet others see students treating the management education learning process as a utilitarian vehicle and not challenging what they learn in management schools.

Now what we must change is the way young people and executives see what management is, what a business school is, and what learning means. To be more down to earth, the students today seem to accept the fact that they will not be able to know everything about everything, so they go to a sort of utilitarian way of acquiring the knowledge for business education, which is a sort of 'I just need to know what I need to know at the moment when I need it, so I am no more thinking about education other than as a stock'.

A particularly strident respondent/critic rails against teaching management as a set of professional disciplines instead of recognising that management is about people issues and leveraging the skills of people in organisations.

The biggest one is not really knowing what is a manager, and thinking educated professional disciplines, like finance, marketing, etc. would make a manager. And that is a complete error. Because when you talk about management it is about bringing people [together] so that they deliver desired results, hopefully for a better good. It does not have to do with marketing and finance and whatever! It is a pure people issue. How much of people issues are in the business school or in the management education of a company?

3.5.1.3. The Holistic Nature of Management The transition to a business school as a school of management focussing on the nature of management, not just functional disciplines, is evident in the following comments:

The biggest challenge is how do you transform yourself, define what a business school is all about and what it should teach?

We need a transformation of that, we need to think really clearly about how to become, a "school for business", where you become a sort of value-adding orchestrator of solutions that businesses need. (Asian respondent)

I think that the job that needs to be done with undergraduates is to prepare them to be properly trained throughout their careers, to be able to absorb knowledge and skills quickly and to be able to deal critically with the flow of information with which they are going to be faced, to be able to do something with this information surfing that they are going to face — I think that it is going to be a totally different world. So we need to prepare them to deal with that effectively. So I am more worried about the skills for learning that we imbue in them than what we make them learn. I think that it will be less important to get an undergraduate to know finance or marketing well than it is to make him or her think critically about almost anything.

It is clear, therefore, that there is a push towards programmes that have a much more integrated and holistic view of the management environment given the huge emphasis on environmental change, sustainable development and the increasing number of corporate scandals across the globe. This is amplified in the following comments:

The leadership challenges, in other words, are very different today. The one fundamental shift is that 10 or 15 years ago the MBA focused largely on the functional aspects of business, finance, accounting, marketing, HR, etc., and maybe a capstone strategy course to try to bring it all together. Today I think that the trends are that though we still need to teach the functional disciplines how do we integrate them more effectively? How do we address the challenges of sustainable development across the various disciplines rather than just add on courses? How do we bolt them on? How do we integrate them effectively?

And if I may perhaps express a big concern about the increasing specialisation in the different business areas from an academic viewpoint, I think we need specialised scholars in different areas. But I think that it is still important that we in the field of management actually try to keep an integrated perspective of what matters and does not matter, what could be relevant and may not be relevant.

3.5.1.4. The Nature of Leadership New paradigms of management education need new leadership approaches, particularly in skills development:

> So the challenge for business communities is really what kind of business leaders will we need in the future to meet the future challenges. And for the business schools, what kind of business leaders do we need to educate? What kind of capabilities and skills will they need to meet these future challenges?

> So what I see emerging is that schools (like the ones we are accustomed to) need to focus more on management development, particularly the skills component. And treat the content as something that students can pick up in a variety of ways. That's part of that process. I think that what we've learned is that doing skills development — leadership development, communication, creative thinking — is really hard and we need to get better at doing them.

There is also a renewed stress on leading people in complex, and sometimes virtual, environments.

> Leading people has new complexity. On the one hand is the issue of horizontally influencing colleagues who don't like to follow, who want to be treated as peers. On the other hand, the workforce is now so diverse that how can you lead [it]? How do you lead virtual units? How do you lead ageing workforces? The diversity is just making this people issue so important.

3.5.1.5. The Pressure of Stakeholders The increasing influence of stakeholder perspectives and management is increasingly evident in the responses.

> Philosophically, I think the biggest challenge is that we have been so successful over the last 20 years ... that we think that business education is about marketing, strategy, operations, finance, whatever. And that in doing so we do not necessarily answer the questions of companies anymore-I mean their needs in terms of social responsibility and coping with environmental issues.

This is reinforced by a renewed focus on the relationship between business, government and society.

> [The challenge for society] is to find its footing in the sense of how society is brought to play a role again in business, in a genuine way. I think that a lot of it at the moment is just going for fashionable things, such as CSR and things like that. Half of [managers] may believe in it but the other half does it because they feel that have to.

> Finally there is a point that has to do with management and has also to do with the corporate world in general, which is how we think about the role of companies in society, how we think about the role of senior executives in companies and societies. I am not thinking about the functional perspectives of the role of business leaders, mainly about how those people generate the respect and [how] their function goes beyond value creation or wealth accumulation and has some type of social purpose that goes beyond making somebody richer.

3.5.1.6. The Influence of Crisis Normally, behaviour and change in organisations is strongly influenced by the presence of crisis conditions. Yet in the context of management education there is a feeling that business schools have adopted a posture of inertia.

> [We] have had a number of crises and I don't think that we have prepared business people to think about these broadly enough. … What really worries me is that business schools still seem to think that what they taught in the past is fine.

3.5.1.7. Moral and Ethical Perspectives The other strong view is that business schools have not provided the necessary insights about moral and ethical responsibility to ensure effective managerial conduct in crises.

> The problem of this crisis is not a problem of knowledge; it is a problem of conduct.

> So it is not that people didn't understand finance, strategy, profit and loss accounts and mortgages. It is that people were negligent and people were greedy. People were lying. So they call it, euphemistically, lack of transparency; but it is pure lying.

People have to modify their conduct. It is even more than purely ethics so to speak, it is behaviour. And, therefore, I believe that business schools ... should emphasise that the great challenge of management education in the future is emphasising conduct more than knowledge and skills.

3.5.1.8.   The Role and Value of Research   Several respondents question the value of management research for a managerial audience:

> The legitimacy of our research struck me most, sitting around a table with the other actors in social science, questioning the legitimacy of our research and not being impressed.

> I don't think that management schools and management research ask particularly interesting research questions. It's noticeable, particularly in Europe, that those who are probably best placed to argue and comment — and asked for comments — on social and economic problems in society, which would range from climate change to politics to inequality to the whole diverse range of financial meltdown, are very rarely academics from business schools.

The key challenge is seen as the balance between theory and practice in managerial research.

> The biggest ongoing challenges have been around for about 100 years and they're still there. Which is how do you balance scholarly research and endeavour from a high-quality academic point of view with the need to train and develop a large number of professionals?

3.5.1.9.   Rigour/Relevance   This is also often described as the rigour/relevance dilemma in managerial research.

> The one thing is the balance of academic and professional engagement. You know what seems to me has happened is that hopefully as a consequence of the Gordon and Howell report of 1959 we've invested pretty heavily to make business education more academic. And we've been quite successful at doing that. And AACSB accreditation, I think, reflects that. But the question about whether we've gone too far, whether the pendulum has swung too far, is really a relevant question in two ways. One is sort of for the average business school

whether the mean is too far towards the academic and not enough towards practice. The other is the extreme, whether the business school is a legitimate business school without a significant emphasis on practice.

In the British and Australasian contexts there is a questioning of the so-called research assessment exercises (RAE), which have had the effect of forcing management education to be much more academic in orientation.

The biggest challenge I have is the government-imposed RAE or equivalent that pushes my faculty towards anything but relevance and impact.

Some of the academics that are around don't really understand the business world they're talking about.

I think that one of the reasons that a lot of the research that is being done by business schools is viewed by the corporates as not useful is that they can't understand it. Therefore, CEOs say why should I have these people come and teach the people in my company if this is what they are going to teach them. And I think that that is the greatest problem.

I think that we still need research-and rigorous research. But I think that the issue of relevance and how we make it relevant is very important.

3.5.1.10. Impact of Management Education   In summary, management education research is seen to have little impact.

We spend far too much time being far too clever (in research) with far too little impact.

3.5.1.11. Link/Balance to Practice   Many respondents stress the critical importance of management education and research in order to ensure a balanced linkage to practice.

I think there is a continuing challenge of relevance. There is a phenomenon that I think child psychologists call parallel play. There is a certain age of children where if you put them in a room with toys, they play alongside each other rather than with each other, I think it's between two and four. And I think that you can observe parallel play in the business-academic world in that too often I've seen a stream of activity that goes into universities and researchers talking to each other and working within their own worlds, and the business

community working within its own world, and only occasion-
ally do the two cross over and meet.

3.5.2. External Conditions Confronting the Management Education Industry

Respondents perceive a consistent set of external challenges to management
education including globalisation and the economic/cultural aspects of
competition.

3.5.2.1. Globalisation The influence of globalisation is seen on the one
hand as self-evident but on the other hand as challenging in providing, for
example, the resources/cases to produce a well-rounded, globally aware
student.

Comments about the contents of globalisation approaches follow:

> Globalisation in terms of the resources for schools that plan to
> exploit opportunities beyond [their] border ... will require
> them to engage in alliances with other schools and also in
> trying to participate in knowledge creation and research in
> order to have a rather more cosmopolitan understanding of
> developments in parts of the world. That's a major stretch
> for people who focus much more on research.

> Another challenge is how business schools actually cope with
> the new realities of the business world. I see the cross-cultural
> dimensions of managing today as more important than ever.
> I think that we haven't yet realised, at least in the west, how
> important those things are, particularly the learning, not the
> teaching, about management in a global environment.

But the importance of inculcating a sense of global and cultural
intelligence in students is seen as very critical.

> The biggest challenge — and I don't think that any of the
> other challenges come close to it — is that of building a
> capable person to operate effectively in a global context — a
> go-anywhere graduate. It is such a challenge because that is
> what business needs but it's a bigger challenge because schools
> tend to be institutions in their particular environments and
> even sub-divided into their disciplines. They are not building
> a composite individual; they are building people through
> separate disciplines and different emphases. Business schools
> hope that it pastes and hangs together in the end.

> On a wider front I think the challenge for management education is becoming very much a global and international activity. I think there's competition emerging for which institution can actually understand how to do it well internationally.

The overall challenge is also seen to be to existing models of management education, particularly the US/European model.

> At the same time, because the world's becoming global there's a clash, a challenge to the perceived Anglo-American model.

3.5.2.2. Competition In the competitive context of management education the following trends are seen:

> Massive competition in certain areas. The volatility of the global economy and the diversity of approaches to economic development worldwide. Nobody knows exactly how to tackle these issues. And the third additional change is the growing competition from private initiatives.

> In the area of private competition, I think that there is a growing challenge by people like Apollo (the University of Phoenix) in some ways, but also I think that tomorrow there w[ill] be real pressure from the Tatas and NIAT in India, which come in with a very different model of what business education is all about. That's going to be very tough for our existing financial models.

However, some question the strength of private competition:

> I'm not sure whether the threat from the for-profit business school world is going to be that strong, but it might be. Some people say that it will be because it will give people what they want, without paying for what they don't want, which is research.

Others see it as a real challenge:

> What I figure is happening is that there's a bit of a fault line developing in business education and that the competition for doing business education is, I think, emerging, so that a lot of the content-based management education is increasingly able to be provided by a variety of for-profit as well as existing organisations.

3.5.3. *Internal Conditions Confronting the Management Education Industry*

There are also seen to be a wide range of internal challenges for management education centred on the role of faculty quality, the funding of management education and the development of new models of management education.

3.5.3.1. Role of Faculty The universities, and faculty, are seen to be a significant impedance to the growth of management education.

> In the context of the universities, there's still a lack of dialogue between business schools and corporations. When I go around the world talking to business schools and I say something like 'do you have a corporate advisory board?' some will say no. I am still amazed that there's an ivory tower mentality in some of the business schools.

Faculty cultures and practices, including tenure, are seen as challenges and difficult issues to handle.

> I think that the whole question of tenure needs to be raised because you've got some pretty old people out there.

> I think that the snobbery of academia is not helpful. I think great teachers should be recognised and revered as much, if not more, than great researchers because I think that they have a longer-term impact on people.

> A critical cultural practice that is argued to hinder knowledge development is the so-called 'publish/perish' syndrome.

> In the creation of knowledge, I feel that we need some kind of evolutionary reform, or even close to a revolution, which is not going to be easy because of the way academia traditionally works from an administrative point of view. If you want to prosper in this academic endeavour; basically what you have to do is publish or perish.

> I think that there is an ongoing challenge by the fact that the evaluation system re faculty is so strongly determined by research performance, not in terms of what is useful research but in terms of what will get into journals. Yet that's not meeting the actual demand for pedagogy and providing people with the ability to have the right teachers in front of the students.

On the other hand, there may indeed be a shortage of high-quality faculty.

> Now very important to me is the issue of quality faculty and faculty recruitment. The job market for faculty has globalised so that salaries are globalised as well. And that creates significant cost pressures for schools that have a significant revenue stream based on their domestic markets. And that creates a mismatch.

3.5.3.2. Funding and Revenue Models   Allied to the need to hire and recruit faculty is the ability to build sustainable financial models for management education.

> The biggest challenges are financial. The executive education market collapsed in the recession. Nobody yet knows how it's going to shape up in the future. This is a big chunk of income for many schools.

> Degree programmes have probably reached their limit in terms of what can be charged and there will be renewed price resistance. In the past the market has seemed price inelastic but I suspect that this is coming to an end.

All in all there is a clear view that the current financial model of business schools will be hard to sustain in the future.

> The business of business education is changing. Because of the pressure, we are all chasing full-time MBA classes as the pinnacle of what we should be doing. In the UK, 93% of full-time MBA students are not from the UK and lots of really good schools, including ourselves, have trouble recruiting decent-size classes of MBAs. Therefore how to make ends meet in a business school in appropriate ways is a big challenge.

> All of these issues focus on the resource base of the schools. Developing a stronger resource basis for endowments is also important. However, philanthropy and fund-raising aren't so well-established, so this is a major challenge.

> Overall, management education is going through enormous change. Where will the new revenue streams come from to

put the school at the cutting edge? There is a clear need for investment in high-quality faculty based on the school's mission. To summarise, challenges in UK management education are to survive the radical restructuring with increased competition and increased fees. Some universities such as Sussex, Exeter, Lancaster and Surrey are betting on the growth of management education.

3.5.3.3. New Models of Management Education The funding and faculty challenges have heightened the need to explore newer, more innovative and perhaps more effective models of management education.

> I think that adults learn differently today than they did before. The idea of the classroom as the focal point of the learning is, I think, an obsolete idea, and it's not like we will continue to do case studies and do group work, it is much more like how do you redesign lifelong learning in such a way that it takes into account the possibilities of the internet and information/ communication technologies. So I think that that is an additional challenge for business schools — to change the way in which adults learn.

As noted earlier, crises can also influence new model development.

> I think the financial crisis was a massive wake-up call. It showed very clearly that the segmentation and fragmentation of management education, with finance people not knowing everything about human behaviour and probably knowing very little about organisation, was a real problem.
> We need to develop a diversifying model in a culturally, sensitive manner. There is a need for a new business model(s). The US model is at centre stage but there needs to be a blending between Europe (Grande Ecole) and US models.

Some of the key elements in new models of management education include the following:

> I think that other questions are how is technology going to change and how do business schools that rely strongly on face-to-face teaching (which are often the premium business schools) continue to justify their existence when you now can get such high-quality teaching and information through on-line channels. How do you still maintain your distinctiveness?

And there is continuing questioning about the value of the MBA.

> In about 1985 or maybe 1988, *BusinessWeek* had an article about the death of the MBA and I swear if you go back and look, they run articles every five to eight years that the MBA is dead. Part of me thinks that maybe it's just topical and it's nice to take big swings at the MBA because it's a popular thing to criticise but one of these times it may actually be dead. So it's the issue of what to actually do about that ... let alone the Executive MBA ... we're looking at that as well.

Another respondent wondered whether the MBA would be cannibalised by the new Masters of Management degree:

> I wonder if the Masters in Management degree has undermined the MBA in some ways. Companies wanting to hire younger people. The classic MBA person of 27–28 has become a "rough model." I don't know whether the Masters in Management will take the place of the MBA in terms of numbers but I do sense a change in thinking.

One respondent talked clearly about model transitions:

> I think that we need to think about a transition from the old model to a new model:

> The old model: faculty meetings, departments, tenured-based vested interests. These all add up to making it not very credible that these types of organisations will be able to adapt to a demand-side orientation. I am sorry to say it but I think that we probably need to get rid of some of this old approach.

> To create a new model we need to get rid of some over-conservative, narrow-minded ways of thinking. I think that the role of traditional management disciplines like marketing, finance, etc. is quite clear but the world is growing asymmetrically and we really need to think about innovation and change in different ways. And my feeling is that the next wave of innovation will come from Asia. We need an innovative perspective and to make it happen there has to be a willingness to experiment. That's what I would like to see more of.

Another respondent noted the influence of innovation on the development of network-type organisations:

> Open sourcing and open innovation in an enterprise in 2020 will change. I don't know if business schools know that

perhaps in 15 years there may not be such a thing as a manager any more in some parts of business. You become a node in the network. The interesting point is how do you become a relevant node in the network and designing/ understanding how network organisations work.

3.5.4. Summary and Conclusions

Reviewing EFMD's profile over the last 40 years it is apparent that as a professional management education association it has achieved and established a clear identity. Distinctive aspects of this identity include its strong network of both corporate and academic members (extending to its governance structure) and its important international/global footprint promoting management education outside Europe, particularly, in Asia, Africa and the Middle East. Its mantra has been to ensure quality management education through both accreditation and sponsorship of research but with a focus on social democratic models of capitalism that stress stakeholder perspectives including corporate social responsibility and sustainability.

Those leading management educators who led EFMD in its first 25 years also stressed EFMD's catalytic role in promoting educational innovation, involving such issues as invoking principles of liberal management education and recognising the impacts of both globalisation and the pace of technological and social change. They emphasised the need to embrace change, avoid complacency and inertia, and develop alternative approaches, paradigms and models in management education in the new era of innovation and change.

The media have continued to question the role and value of management education. They regularly address the value of the MBA and question whether business schools have taken the lead in educating students about the need for a proper ethical and moral compass in management tasks and in building a proper awareness of international relations, globalisation and contextual/cultural intelligence. In short, they are sceptical about business schools and do not understand why teaching approaches have not better addressed the impacts of the Internet, and new information/communication technologies.

What is interesting and important about our interviewees is that they believe that management education has not faced up to the challenges of its value and relevance. Stakeholders question why it continues to use the same old model and the role, value, quality and legitimacy of both management education and management research. The sense is that many of the ongoing challenges — perceptual, external and internal — remain and that new models have been slow to emerge. In essence, management education is seen as reactive, lacking innovation and possessing too much evidence of complacency and incremental change. We will examine these issues further.

Chapter 4

The Key Stakeholders in Management Education

4.1. Who Are the Most Important Stakeholders in Management Education?

At the centre of the criticisms and challenges facing management education is an apparent disconnect between the role of business schools and the expectations and experiences of stakeholders. We asked respondents who they consider key stakeholders to be, which stakeholder has the greatest influence and identify the role of their own stakeholder group.

These are questions that are implicitly raised by critics of and commentators on management education. For example, the criticism that management research is irrelevant contains a substantial disconnect between stakeholders — for whom should management research be relevant and why? Despite this, rarely is the management education community asked directly to discuss the position and role of its own stakeholders. There is therefore a clear need to understand better the roles and needs of stakeholders in management education and to embrace stakeholder management perspectives in management education. (A mapping of the set of potential stakeholders in management education is shown in Figure 4.1. This provides a framework to anchor our subsequent discussion of key stakeholders.)

The first question asked was: 'Who do you consider to be the key stakeholders in management education?' Where possible, respondents were also asked to rank key stakeholders by their relative importance within management education.

4.2. Who Do You Consider the Key Stakeholders in Management Education?

Table 4.1 shows the most frequently used terms by respondents to describe stakeholders. This list should be compared with Table 4.2, which shows the ranking of key stakeholders by respondents.

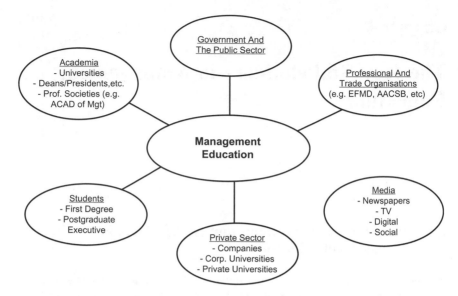

Figure 4.1: Sources of influence on management education.

Table 4.1: Frequency of themes related to key stakeholders.

Word	Count
business/businesses/companies/organisations	108
manager/manager(s)/management/managing	78
student/students	66
people	50
education/educating/educate	48
faculty	29
society	24
university/universities	22
employ/employability/employed/employer(s)/employment	21
government(s)	20
community/communities	17
world	16
learn/learning	13
economics/economists	12
corporate/corporation(s)/corporatize	11
individual(s)	11
market/marketing	11

Table 4.1: (*Continued*)

Word	Count
programme(s)	10
teach/teaching/teachers	10
consumer/consuming	9
develop/developing/development	9
funders/funding/funded/fundraising/funds	9
graduate(s)	9

More specifically, Table 4.1 shows the top stakeholder themes identified by the respondents, whereas Table 4.2 clearly identifies students as the most important stakeholders in management education with about half of the respondents placing them first. However, this outcome is not as clear-cut as it first appears. Indeed, this question prompted much critical reflection by respondents and an analysis of the interview data reveals underlying issues, and sources of confusion, in identifying key stakeholders.

For example, when we asked respondents whom the key stakeholders are in management education, they typically gave one of two responses. The first is a 'pragmatic' assessment that contrasts who *should* be a key stakeholder with which stakeholder groups are currently best served by management education. The second response draws a distinction between the types of student involvement in management education, and specifically focuses on whether the stakeholders are involved purely in executive education or in all aspects of management education. A subset of the population believes that there are different (possibly conflicting) stakeholders for executive education as compared with management education more generally.

4.3.   Should Students Be Key Stakeholders?

First, it is clear that the majority of interviewees believe that students should be the key stakeholders since they are the principal consumers of management education. They suggest that students should be 'top of the pile' yet also assert that this may not always be the case. One North American respondent articulates this problem in the following terms:

> Well, I always think that I'm supposed to say business because they pay the bills for the students but I really think that the key

Table 4.2: Summary of ranking of key stakeholders in management education.

	Students (%)	Organisations/ Business (%)	Employers (%)	Faculty (%)	University (%)	Others (%)	Government (%)	Society (%)
First	46	17	11	6	3	0	6	11
Second	26	17	14	9	6	6	9	0
Third	6	17	6	11	11	14	3	3
First and second	72	34	25	14	9	6	14	11
Top three	78	51	31	26	20	20	17	14

Thirty-five out of 36 respondents gave discernible rankings of importance to stakeholders.
Using the ranking of key stakeholders by respondents, we get the above picture — students feature in the top three ranking of stakeholders for over three-quarters of our respondents. Just under half position students as the number-one stakeholder in management education.

stakeholders are the students, it's their life. Business *is* an important stakeholder — they want quality graduates. But the students want careers that are enriched and motivating. They want to come to work every day. I think they're the key stakeholders; they have to be listened to but sometimes you have to listen and throw the ball a little further down-field ... to make them look at what will make them happy in the long run.

Other respondents stress the conflicts for business schools in their role as academic institutions on the one hand and 'commercial businesses' on the other. They question how they balance academic and commercial values:

You'd think that in order of priority it should be students and employers at the top, university and the communities that they are part of, and then faculty but I think that it doesn't always work out that way in practice.

It leads to an academic dilemma because if you treat the student as a customer then you are compromising the academic side of the business. On the other hand, you may have to treat them as a customer to satisfy the other stakeholders, i.e. companies. Somehow they [business schools] have to balance the idea of being academic institutions but also being businesses that are selling bodies to companies and without the ability to do that can't sustain themselves financially. It's a big problem — how are they going to work that out?

In addition, students also figure as key stakeholders because of the relationship between business as consumers of skilled graduates and business schools as suppliers of this resource. As such, businesses and employers emerge among the foremost stakeholders because of their position in the labour market as customers seeking skilled managers. This perception of management education as a supply-chain arrangement reinforces the position of students at the very core of management education. This maintains the view that business schools must serve to develop skilled individuals who provide significant added value to business.

This latter viewpoint summarises the constant tensions between teaching and research with what amounts to a balancing act — an academic dilemma — for business schools to negotiate. Is it still the case that business school deans continue to enact Steven Kerr's (1975) notorious folly of hoping for excellence in teaching while rewarding research activity? Certainly, the evidence from the ground shows that students are not key stakeholders and it appears that the problem described by Kerr persists.

Other respondents illustrate the tensions that exist with business schools often being seen as 'advocates' for business, resulting in an unbalanced and unethical perspective on business's role in society.

> Don't be a prostitute of business. I have been disgusted for many years about how business school professors wrote case studies just for heroic CEOs and how they became gurus of the ones in power.

> What I also deeply criticise is the incestuous relationship that many schools have to the finance and consulting industry, especially on MBA programmes. [The] minimalistic reduction of management to finance, and even to a specific part of finance, is connected with financial capitalism.

4.4. Distinguishing Between Types of Students Reveals Different Perceptions of the Relative Importance of Key Stakeholders

A further insight from our data suggests that the relative importance of stakeholders is contingent on the type of student in question. Students become increasingly important stakeholders, particularly where companies become involved in executive education.

> There is the education of people for a job, which is the role of post-graduate executive education. There I think that the key stakeholders are the companies. … And then there is educating younger people, and there I think that the key stakeholder is society and the individual.

Indeed, throughout the interviews it was common for respondents to say 'it depends on what kind of student' and the answer above illustrates how divergent or conflicting stakeholder interests might exist in management education. As another interviewee remarked 'it depends what the product is' and that there are both 'business to business' (b2b) and 'business to consumer' (b2c) activities in business schools.

This is expressed in the following terms:

> I think that it depends a little bit on what the product is. I think there are business to business and business to consumer activities within business schools. The business to consumer ones are the undergraduate [and] postgraduate courses, as it were, and perhaps the short courses where the key stakeholder is actually the client paying for that particular product. So if it's for the MBA, it's the MBA student, rather than the corporation that's going to hire them. I think that we are in dangerous territory right now between global business education and some of the nonsense coming out of the UK government, which wants to directly correlate education to employability and to a job. I think this is just the wrong way to go, because it [the business school] is not a vocational school for immediate after-graduation roles; it should surely be something that is more academic and thoughtful and broad.

Therefore, determining the key stakeholder is again contingent on the kind of student or customer involved. Generally executive courses are perceived as a b2b proposition, with business schools providing a service to the businesses that employ graduates. Undergraduates, postgraduate and doctoral studies represent a b2c arrangement where key stakeholders are the students themselves and increasingly are subject to broader concerns such as their contribution to society. Clearly, students are an extremely important stakeholder, both from an employer and a customer perspective.

4.5. Which Stakeholders Have Had the Greatest Influence on Management Education Over the Last 20 Years?

To assess the relative influence of the range of stakeholders, interviewees were asked which stakeholders have had the greatest influence on management education over the last 20 years and, where possible, to rank the influence of these stakeholders.

Table 4.3 shows that business schools, their faculty, companies/business/ industry and students are the most frequently mentioned stakeholders that have had the greatest influence on management education over the last 20 years. This ranking of influential stakeholders by interviewees in Tables 4.4(a) and 4.4(b) presents an interesting contrast to the viewpoint that identifies students as the key stakeholder group.

Table 4.3: Frequency of stakeholder themes mentioned (indications of influence).

Word	Count	Similar words
business schools	40	school, schools
faculty	35	faculty, educators
companies/business/industry	34	
students	32	student, students
education	29	educated, education
change	29	change, changed, changes, changing
managing	24	manage, manageable, management, managing
programmes	21	programme, programmes
influence	20	influence, influenced, influences
universities	16	universities, university
research	14	research, researchers
rankings	13	ranked, rankings
stakeholders	9	stakeholder, stakeholders
impact	9	impact, impacts
learns	9	learned, learning, learns
teaching	9	teach, teaching
corporate	8	corporate, corporates, corporations
countries	8	countries, country
degree	8	degree
demand	8	demand, demands
development	8	developed, developing, development
executive	8	executive
graduate	8	graduate, graduates, graduating

Table 4.4(a): Ranking: Which stakeholders have had the greatest influence on management education over the last 20 years?

	Faculty	Business	Students	Auditors	Government	No one	Rankings	Business schools	Accreditors	Media	Deans/Leaders	Recruiters	Alumni	CEOs	Public institutions	European schools
First	15	9	5	1	1	1	1	1	1	0	0	0	0	0	0	0
Second	2	1	1	0	0	0	2	2	0	2	1	1	1	1	1	1
Third		1	1													

Table 4.4(b): Summary of most influential stakeholders in management education by ranking.

	Faculty	Business	Students	Auditors	Government	No one	Rankings	Business schools	Accreditors	Media	Deans/Leaders	Recruiters	Alumni	CEOs	Public institutions	European schools
First	43%	26%	14%	3%	3%	3%	3%	3%	3%	0%	0%	0%	0%	0%	0%	0%
Second	6%	3%	3%	0%	0%	0%	6%	6%	0%	6%	3%	3%	3%	3%	3%	3%
First or Second	49%	29%	17%	3%	3%	3%	9%	9%	3%	6%	3%	3%	3%	3%	3%	3%
Top three	49%	31%	20%	3%	3%	3%	9%	9%	3%	6%	3%	3%	3%	3%	3%	3%

In terms of those who have influenced management education in the last 20 years, faculty, business (business generally and as 'consumers') and students emerge as the most influential.

This corresponds to two broad alternative perspectives on management education over the last 20 years. The first is a *supply-driven perspective* where the preferences, terms and conditions of employment and institutional factors mean that faculty are in charge and determine what is taught to students and which areas of research are pursued. This puts faculty in position as the most influential stakeholders. An alternative perspective corresponds to a *demand-driven perspective* where either students or business are perceived as most influential in shaping management education.

4.6.   Influence Over Management Education as a Supply-Driven Phenomenon

With faculty clearly dominant in terms of their influence over management education and yet students deemed to be a key stakeholder, it is inviting to envisage the *Gravy Training* scenario outlined by Crainer and Dearlove (1998) where the relevance of student training comes second to the pursuits of faculty in their ivory towers.

Our data contains examples of faculty's influence in the running and direction of business schools. Tenured faculty are seen as controlling the agenda, the curricula and governance mechanisms in business schools:

> Faculty [are a strong influence], because they control the business schools. They control the business schools by the tenure process, you get them in, you can never get them out. Once they're in they're basically free to do what they want. They can block any change in [a] school.

Faculty also set the agenda and drive change:

> The faculty ... have historically defined what is taught, when subjects need to change and how they need to change. They are the dynamic drivers of change.

Faculty are also perceived to emphasise research over teaching and do not connect with end-users (business):

> Because they design the programmes, they influence the way in which management education has moved very much into a research-obsessed situation. For me, teaching has become very, very secondary to research.

> Most of the changes have come internally — [via] faculty —
> who are not always well-connected to the end-users.

And, tenure creates a governance process in which faculty have considerable power and influence:

> Faculty are at the front lines of management education and in
> many institutions there's a tradition of family governance ...
> and they wield a fair amount of decision-making power in
> some ways because of things like tenure. I think that they've
> been most influential.

4.7. Influence Over Management Education as a Demand-Driven Phenomenon

What also emerges from the data is an indication that both business and students are perceived as playing a highly influential role in management education. It is this that forms a demand-driven perception of management education. This was especially evident in executive and post-experience courses, possibly because stakeholder interests are much more closely aligned where each student is a *de facto* representative of business as both an employee and agent of business. Therefore, within a demand-driven form, the sphere of influence shifts from within academia and is led by consumer demand from student and business stakeholders.

Under this scenario the mechanisms of influence for students are that they pay fees — as one respondent commented 'extortionate fees'. This means that they are positioned to influence *how* and *where* courses are delivered and also express demand for specific course content (e.g. finance, management accounting and consultancy skills).

Similarly, businesses are seen to be in an influential position either because, like students, they are paying for management education for their staff or prospective staff. It is therefore likely that businesses, following the trials of the global financial crisis and their relative importance in funding higher education, will increasingly influence the agenda and swing the balance of power from the state and academic constituencies.

Another mechanism that allows businesses to have a role in driving the classroom agenda is in terms of the kinds of skills and expertise expected from business school graduates. As the ultimate 'consumer', businesses have influence by *demanding* employable graduates and the skills they should have (e.g. CSR, ethics, sustainability, negotiation and decision making or knowledge management). In a climate of economic recession and a general trend of state austerity that is reducing or freezing funding for higher education, the bargaining power of fee-paying students and businesses strengthens. We should expect the relative influence of students and businesses to increase as they push for value-for-money from management education and pay the bills for business schools.

Students are seen to have an increasing influence, and market power, on the conduct of business schools:

> Students, in the sense that they have the market power because of over-supply in certain areas, have influenced business schools to become much more business oriented. We are 90% privately funded now, so we run much more like business. ... We have to listen to our "customers" because I think that students do have a customer hat.

Students are also increasingly aware of educational costs.

> I think that it's the increasing demand of their students for schools to justify the exorbitant fees they are charging. So there's definitely been a trend to seeing a student as a customer, both in the eyes of the school and the eyes of the student. I have certainly had comments, last year, that the students knew exactly what their per-hour cost was. ... So they're pretty clear, aren't they — they're there to be entertained and to get a job.

4.8. Other External Influences

The rich interview data and our own experiences reveal that much has changed in management education in the 14 years since Crainer and Dearlove's wake-up call. Globalisation, advances in information technology, a continued growth in student numbers, the prominence and expansion of accreditation bodies as well as an increasing focus on performance in rankings are all driving changes in the relationships and influence of stakeholders.

It is somewhat surprising that media and professional organisations have not featured highly in the perceptions of our interviewees as influential stakeholders. Both rankings and auditors are seen as influential stakeholder groups by a small number of respondents yet this effect is far less than for faculty, students and business. The comparatively low perceived influence of rankings and auditors tells only part of the story; there is a link between these stakeholders and the supply- and demand-driven models of management education discussed earlier.

On the one hand, rankings have continued to follow the customer by, for example, providing information on average earnings and the number of alumni in employment. This reinforces the shift of influence over courses and education towards students or, at least, away from faculty. On the other hand, the concerns of auditors such as EQUIS and AACSB appear more closely aligned with a supply-driven model with their concerns anchored in academic quality.

However, many deans and university administrators view rankings as an increasingly important signal of the reputation of management education. The tyranny of rankings, as Rakesh Khurana has consistently argued, has a dysfunctional relationship with management education by focusing attention on things like the increase in earnings of graduates or school image rather than either academic concerns or the need for problem solving by businesses.

One respondent stresses the homogenising influence of external auditors in setting standards for both research and teaching outputs and quality.

> I would argue the external auditors. I think that what's happened is that research has suffered greatly. For example, I find it very difficult to flip through a copy of almost any journal now — and I receive a whole load of them — and find anything of any interest or relevance. Now that could be a function of my age and that I've seen it all before but I think that what's happening is that there's a very strong game going on, which is simply driven by those external auditors.' 'QA (quality assurance) type assessments have been strong across the UK but less so across continental Europe. What that has also meant is that a particular approach and supposed standards of teaching have been imposed upon business schools — how to teach MBAs, what is learning and so on. Those have shaped the educational agenda in my view, and I would argue strongly that younger authors and researchers care very much less about the content of what they have published, and very much more about where they publish it, because journals are ranked.

> The focus is on which journals, how many publications and how is that going to get us up in the rankings, either in research and a bit less so in teaching. So there's this homogeneity across Europe of a particular model of education and a particular model of research, and I that if any stakeholder is powerful it is that one ...

The rankings, in particular, are seen as an important performance indicator for business schools:

> I would like to think deans and faculty have influence but unfortunately the popular press and the rankings have had a greater impact on the competitive forces in management education. It used to be the case that a school was considered good based on the quality of its PhD students but it's now judged on rankings and that effects how resources are allocated, so no resources are given to doctoral education. This is different from some other areas of academia where there's money for PhD students but no real demand for them. We have a huge demand for them but produce very few. ... The media have forced changes in strategy that are not consistent with the quality of research ...

4.9. What Do You See as the Role of Your Stakeholder Group in Management Education?

We asked interviewees to specify the role of their own stakeholder group in management education. Some interviewees, however, talked about management education in general while others, in a more straightforward manner, addressed their own stakeholder group roles more directly.

The four stakeholder groups (media, business, professional/trade, academics) broadly unite around a common calling, or goal, for their stakeholder group. This hinges on the perceived need to *bridge, communicate across* or *reduce* the gap between management research (and, by implication, teaching in business schools) and what managers do. Around this commonly held mission, there are more nuanced roles and purposes developed by the four stakeholder groups.

4.10. Media

The media regards itself as having a deeply ingrained position, largely through the importance and popularity of its rankings of schools. However, while it perceives similar hurdles as other stakeholders, it regards itself as having an arms-length role through providing 'objective' information and informing groups of people where previously there was a lack of information about management education. They argue that rankings are objective and are consistent in their choice of performance measures. They view rankings as a service to business schools as mid-ranking schools emerge 'in the same sphere as the top schools and in the range of the top 100'. Rankings are therefore perceived as objective and as providing a rich source of information to demystify management education to consumers (to the media, this is typically students).

As one UK-based interviewee put it: '[Ranking] does the lower schools much more good than it does the higher ranking schools'.

4.11. Business

Business stakeholders tended to discuss the role of management education rather than their own role in relation to it. From their responses there was a clear logic in their argument that management education needs to change in order to become more relevant for business. This proposition sets the role of the business school, first, as that of a translator between its own research and its customers — businesses — and then in strategic execution to confront and solve business problems using their research-based concepts and techniques. Building on the processes of translation and problem solving, it is then the role of schools to disseminate important 'facts' and improved processes about business innovations to improve the quality of business decisions.

4.11.1. The Issue of Translation

To achieve the role of translator, respondents identified three important developments and directions that they believe management education must take. First, business school research is too narrow. Businesses say that they perceive management research as high quality but as too complex and too far from use and therefore too difficult to apply to the problems faced by businesses. Thus, some kind of translation of narrow research into something that managers can 'do' or use is encouraged.

Second, the issue of translation is impeded by the knowledge gap between academics and managers. They see that the central problem is for management educators to better understand business. Academics are perceived as on the outside looking in, which means that they do not understand the business core:

> The first thing is to understand the real problems of real business. Understanding, understanding, understanding.

> Not ... all faculty members have a good understanding of
> what is going on in businesses. ... I believe that PhDs
> and other educational programmes for faculty have to be
> revisited. Because they have to have a good understanding of
> the world within which they are working and which
> they wish to transform through education. You cannot
> transform the outside world without understanding it. It's
> nonsense.

Third, they stress that it is academics' role to understand and integrate
their research into challenges facing businesses ('understanding the trends
that are shaping the world'), not least the influence of technology:

> People that [understand] the changes in information tech-
> nologies are having the impact they are having in busi-
> ness [because of their level of understanding].

Furthermore, respondents note that the people that understand the core
of business and its relationship with IT are often the most successful
teachers:

> They can go any place in the world and really maintain the
> interest of any manager of any company in the world because
> they really understand what the problems are.

Translation, therefore, consists of the following main elements:

1. Understanding the core business
2. Translating from narrow to broad perspectives by understanding
   the business environment and, crucially, the current trends and issues
   (particularly in the IT domain).

4.11.2.   Problem Diagnosis

A second major issue is for business schools to be in a position to better
diagnose management problems (something that management education is
not currently positioned to do):

> It's like a medical doctor. You go to the doctor because
> you have problems with your prostate or whatever but they
> don't look only at one thing, they look at everything. They

take a blood test and get a medical history from you. Increasingly, doctors understand how to integrate the different problems and give you the right answer. It's very similar to this for business school teachers as, first 'understanding your patient' for a professor is to both understand the problems and how to integrate the particular problems in the larger organisation.

4.11.3. Integrating Translation and Problem Diagnosis

By integrating translation and problem diagnosis, management education should then be in a position to better disseminate 'business facts' to business. If business schools are studying the most innovative firms, the top schools' role is to teach these facts:

> In the case of management, these are the most innovative firms, so I think that in these days, the role for the top schools, the top research schools, is really about disseminating facts; namely, those important non-technological management innovations, to the rest of the world.

Table 4.5 illustrates the need to build the role of management education clearly, breaking down the barriers in translation and improving the relationship between academia and business.

Table 4.5: Translation: The trinity of diagnosis, integration and dissemination.

Roles	Barriers
Translation	Narrow research
Problem solver/ diagnosis	Lack of integration between research and business
Dissemination of 'facts'	Lack of understanding of the 'business core'
	Lack of understanding of challenges faced by business
	Research is 'backward-looking' producing a historical account that is only part of the picture

4.12.   Professional/Trade Bodies

Professional and trade bodies similarly emphasise their role as bridging, or providing a platform, to close the perceived gap between management education and business. Surprisingly, only one respondent saw their role in terms of setting and maintaining quality standards. A concern for professional/trade stakeholders is the problem of research 'looking backwards' to analyse past events rather than examining problem-solving potential in management research. This mirrors what business stakeholders have said.

The main roles of professional bodies are seen as follows:

First, the role of professional/trade bodies is to provide a platform/space/ forum for academia and practice to interact and understand each other:

> Its main role is to provide a platform for discussion and exchange within the business school community and the corporate learning community and also, in an ideal world, bridging these two constituencies.

> [Something] which I still think that we have to do, which I don't think that we are doing well, is serving [as a] bridge between academics and the business world.

Second, respondents regarded it as problematic for trade/professional stakeholders to bridge this academic/corporate divide because of the perceived weaknesses, irrelevance and 'lagging' nature of management research:

> Very often I think that industry and business in general is ahead of academia in practice and so what we end up doing is studying that practice and codifying it, making it transferable, rather than bringing in a brand new idea.

> Usually new things are invented in business and then academia studies it. It tends to perfect it and write about it but we don't have many good stories where academia in business has named/made a cutting-edge direction that business follows and then becomes very successful.

> I really think that if schools worked effectively and collaboratively with other divisions within universities and other partners internationally, that you could find academic institutions getting ahead of business rather than trailing it.

Third, for this group, there is considerable scepticism about how to 'sell' management research and education to managers. In some cases, executive and corporate education becomes shallow and problematic and the gulf between academic research and practice widens:

> When academics started to give their research findings you could just see the eyes of the corporate members just sort of ... thinking what was that ... we've paid for this ... what the hell is he talking about ... how am I going to go back and defend it to the company.

> I see the need for pure academic research but I also worry about how that is actually brought into the classroom, because I think that there's nothing worse than hearing a professor talk about his favourite topic for an entire semester.

They emphasise what they would really like to see from management education:

> If they have a criticism of what we do, we don't actually prepare students in the practice of management ... we don't equip them to practise management. We give them skills, we give them decision-making techniques, we give them all sort of tools from the toolbox but we don't actually teach them to be managers or leaders. And a lot of business schools would say that that is not our job but I think that the employer wants to recruit someone who's going to be good for them, in their place of work, without necessarily giving them a lot more training.

And they go on to specify clear roles and standards:

> The first is what liberal higher education can give you — the ability to analyse, criticise, synthesise, to understand what people are saying, to be articulate in making your own argument and so on.

> Second, a body of knowledge about how organisations work and how they interact with society and their environment so it is all about people in organisations and how people work, and so on. The traditional syllabus, if you like, of the business school.

Third, the key abilities for actually managing — that is to say, the ability to hear what people are saying, the ability to formulate what they might do, how to persuade, how to create order, how to create direction by nudging if necessary, when to bang the table, when not to bang the table.

4.13.   Academics

There is a range of issues that academics see as having an impact on their role in management education. These span issues of who is responsible for teaching as well as conceptual issues that concern the substance and content of management education.

An important observation is that universities no longer have a monopoly on teaching management education:

> Teaching used to be a prerogative of universities, I mean at the tertiary level ... somehow it was a monopoly — other people could teach but the reality is since the beginning of the 19th century with the development of the Humbolt university, teaching at tertiary level had become a monopoly of the universities and they were granted that monopoly by governments in one way or another. That has changed dramatically over the last 10 or 15 years. So teaching is now not something that we have as a monopoly; many other people can teach very well at a lot of private institutions.

Examples of other providers include consultancies, corporate universities, in-house corporate training, and private/for-profits universities such as HULT and the University of Phoenix.

Academics raise again the issues of bridging with practice and the translation of research findings as part of their purpose. Indeed, they frame it almost entirely as their purpose though, this is not what actually happens in management education. However, there are extremely coherent views on what the academic community should be doing in management education:

First, it should bridge the interests of business and academe by solving key important business problems. Second, it should educate strong, well-rounded business leaders for the future (teaching leadership has to date been a weakness in management education).

The gulf between academia and the corporate environment is evident in the following quotes:

> Academia doesn't necessarily know what's going on in corporate life.

> Research leading to teaching is OK if you can encourage progress — that's great. But if we call it a game, the game is this issue of demand-oriented relevance in terms of research and that teaching seems to be under-represented. There's too much of the kind of research that is done because the academicians think that it is important — it is what the lead journals will accept ...

> There's definitely a gulf there between what gets the heavy citations and what gets used — what gets used by students is often not as sophisticated as it ought to be, too much airport literature makes the rounds, too many HBR articles, tremendous simplification. But at the academic end, obfuscation and confusion and words that you cannot read. I collect abstracts and titles of articles I've just read as a kind of amusement. I have no idea what any of the articles are about. That seems a bit funny to me.

The challenges of improving the curriculum and educating future leaders are clearly noted:

> We teach this way because it's the way the curriculum has been for the last 30 or 50 years. This is *my* course; this is *my* article, instead of team teaching and team research.

> I think that the big challenge is how to educate the future business leaders and how to meet the future challenges between the academic and the business world. I think that the faculty should play a key role in this but most of faculty, especially full-time faculty, are trained by the functional discipline based view, which is very narrow, very academic; they don't even know what has happened or what will happen in the business world.

> I think that it is one of the key challenges in business education because that trend to the ever-increasing quantitative

sophistication of our research creates a duality of reward systems. One is for the faculty member's own career and the second is for what I consider personally the more important mission of the institution, which is actually education.

And at least one interviewee questions the reward and incentive structures that stress A-journal research.

I don't think there's an incentive to become applied. Because journals are journals and journals determine careers. Where does the money or the initiative or the value come from for making shorter ... more applied versions of it — because there's great research that gets done but it just gets lost, or it isn't translated ...

However, there is also a strong defence of scholarship, which strengthens the case for translation:

I don't think the actual mix or choice [of disciplines] is important; what I think is important is that academia has a series of core disciplines. I can't disassociate that from the teaching of management and I think that any student who comes out of management without a reasonable understanding of the social, economic, rigorous, quantitative, if you like applied subjects is just missing out. Management is not a free-floating subject. And if it is, it's just froth.

Faculty members have to provide a sense of direction in thinking about future programmes, the future of the educational process itself and about research. So I do think that even the demand side of those outcomes is very important-what companies say, what students say. I still think that that the great scholars can in many ways shape the future of our profession.

Indeed, the quality of faculty is seen as crucial for the creative, future evolution of the business school:

Academics/faculty define the curriculum. The challenge is to get academia to be more responsive to the demands of business and students. We cannot innovate without faculty. We cannot be better than the quality of the faculty.

If one is in a university, research is a *raison d'être* — one of the two major *raisons d'être* for the university. And if one wishes to be in a leading university, it's about a process; it's important to have a process of rigorous inquiry. However, I would just qualify that by saying that it is not about research just for the sake of research.

4.14. Summary and Conclusions

Table 4.6 summarises the important perceived roles of each of the key stakeholders in management education and Table 4.7 gives a flavour of the broad range of opinions offered by selected interviewees from academia, professional organisations, media and business about their roles within management education.

What is evident from the sometimes conflicting viewpoints of the various stakeholders is a refreshing concern to narrow the gap between academia and practice and to encourage the improvement of management and leadership curricula. These questions will be further examined as we focus on issues of change in management education.

Table 4.6: Perceived roles of stakeholder groups in management education.

Stakeholder	Primary perceived role(s)	Other roles
Media	Providing objective information via rankings	Demystification of management education for potential customers
Business	Wants skilled managers and capable leaders from management education	
Professional/ Trade bodies	Bridging, providing an interface between business schools and practice	QA (quality assurance)
Academia	We know what we 'should' be doing, which is the same as the arguments developed earlier that show a normative model of management education to provide skilled managers and good leaders	Research that solves management problems

Table 4.7: The role of your 'own stakeholder group' in management education.

Academia	Professional/Trade Bodies Association	Media	Business
In a sense what we do is sort of take the practice of companies, regurgitate it, reproduce it and say this was an idiosyncratic practice in this particular company but actually it has general value … we basically diffuse management practice from the uniquely successful company into other companies and as such improve the economy as a whole, so there is a very strong diffusion element in there	… its main role is to provide a platform for discussion and exchange within the business school community and the corporate learning community, and also in an ideal world, bridging these two constituencies It is the interface between what is, and what might be. It is the growth engine for developing managers, primarily through the degree process. The key issue for academics is this trying to underpin practice with theory, rather than the other way round. I think that academics who think they develop new ways of doing things in the world are few and far between in business and management — not so	*The role of the media is to provide information — in the 1990s there wasn't much information on management education:* Huge lack of information. And obviously a huge demand for it. Then the rankings came along. They were just a publishing gimmick initially to sell newspapers. But it turned out that the rankings were very much to the business schools' advantage, especially those in the middle range because it put them in the same sphere as the top schools and in the range of the top 100: a case of perception. I think that the media has done business schools some	It should be to provide the link — be a linking-pin. Because I value very, very, highly and feel it's still under-developed — the link between the educational side and the non-educational side, of the membership, so the corporate/business side — which I mean in a wider context — of the EFMD membership

good favours — I don't think that there should be any antagonism in that area. They make good copy. There's always something happening in the business school world that can be written about

true in chemistry for example. Very often I think that industry and business in general is ahead of academia in practice and so what we end up doing is studying that practice and codifying it, making it transferable, rather than bringing in a brand new idea. I think that the finance people said that derivatives came out of academia, and therefore that was theory leading practice, whether that was a good thing in hindsight is another question

... the main role of EFMD, and one that I've always believed in, from when I came to EFMD, but which I still think that we have to do, which I don't think that we are doing well, is serving [as a] bridge between the academics and the business world. And I think this is

We teach this way because it's the way the curriculum has been for the last 30 or 50 years. This is *my* course; this is *my* article instead of team teaching and team research. The very fact that we are writing a book together is bad for you and me, instead of actually writing it alone!

Table 4.7: (*Continued*)

Academia	Professional/Trade Bodies Association	Media	Business
But in terms of the relevance, it is good	because we have never, in the 10 years that I've been there, been able to get the corporate services, the corporate parts off the ground. And in the 10 years that I've been there it really hasn't changed that much. CLIP hasn't done the immense transformation that I think we expected it to do in the corporate services I see the need for pure academic research but I also worry about how that is actually brought into the classroom, because I think that there's nothing worse than hearing a professor talk about his favourite topic for an entire semester		

I think that the big challenge is how to educate the future business leaders and how to meet the future challenges between the academic and the business world. I think that faculty should play a key role in this but most, especially the full-time faculty, are trained by the functional discipline–based view, which is very narrow, very academic; they don't even know that has happened or what will happen in the business world. But after they get PhDs they go to business schools

The student needs are the needs for the real business world, and it is a big challenge for the faculty

... what I think is important is that academia has a series

Table 4.7: (*Continued*)

Academia	Professional/Trade Bodies Association	Media	Business
of core disciplines. I can't disassociate that from the teaching of management, and I think that any student who comes out of a management programme without a reasonable understanding of the social, economic, the rigorous, quantitative, if you like applied subjects is just missing out. Management is not a free-floating subject. And if it is, it's just froth			

Chapter 5

Further Perspectives: What Have Been the Key Events and Innovations in the Evolution of Management Education?

5.1. Introduction

A key question in our research was to ask respondents to identify the most important and significant events in management education over the last 20 years.

Before examining their responses fully we used N-VIVO qualitative analysis to interpret a 'map' of salient themes that could throw light on what respondents are discussing the most. This mapping process identified the following themes (listed in order of frequency of occurrence) as dominant and recurring: globalisation and geography, the roles of students and managers in business schools and management education, accreditation processes, the influence of economic and financial markets (e.g. competition, crises), rankings and the effects of change.

To some extent themes about the role of technology and the MBA merited discussion, though, interestingly, the roles of faculty and governments in management education received much less attention.

5.2. What Are the Most Important Events in Management Education over the Last 20 Years?

Responses to this question cover almost every element captured in Figure 4.1 (stakeholders, government and the competitive environment). The responses (see Table 5.1) are divided by stakeholder region, which allows us to look at similarities and differences between regions.

Table 5.1: Broad evaluation of the most important events in management education over the past 20 years.

Region	Most important events
Asia	• 1990s emergence of European schools (e.g. LBS, INSEAD, IMD) as strong competitors • Reform of the MBA curricula; bringing in Harvard methods and approaches • Globalisation and international trade • Accreditation — as a key mechanism to raise global impact • Rise of Asian schools, e.g. CEIBS • Financial crises and ENRON; lessons for management education • Reunification of Germany; fall of Communism
Europe	• The advent of rankings and accreditation — EQUIS, AACSB and AMBA; the net effect is that the behaviour of 'leading schools' sets a pattern for others to follow • Scandals and crises: dot com bust, financial scandals at ENRON and World Com, financial crash 2007/2008 • Globalisation and emergence of global competition (strength of US and new entrants from Asia) • Stronger voice of, and linkage to, business (particularly on the skill set of employees trained within management education) • Tiananmen Square — a refocusing on human values • Information technology • Development of for-profits, private competition, in the management education sector • The Bologna Process for harmonisation of degrees in the EU • The rise of the MBA
US/Canada	• Challenge to AACSB accreditation from the EQUIS process • Competition between schools and a stronger customer focus • Relevance to business • Technology • Globalisation • Privatisation • Emerging Markets and their growth: East and South • 1990 recession • 9/11 • Only one mention of the Bologna process

Table 5.1: (*Continued*)

Region	Most important events
Australasia	• Exogenous shocks (economic, financial, social technological) to the business environment • Changes in expectations of academics — productivity requirements (A-journal focus) are helping to drive irrelevant research • Globalisation
Other regions	• Corporate scandals and the implied connection to management education made by the media • Social media • Evolution of management education into a life-long learning enterprise with mass appeal

There are many interesting findings in Table 5.1. For example, the Asian responses demonstrate how they have cleverly, and perhaps strategically, observed and imitated the strong growth path of European business schools based on a clear European identity. They have identified European schools as role models for their growth and have subsequently used accreditation, both AACSB and EQUIS, to establish their competitive strength and emphasise their global economic importance and global impact in the development of management education. US business school role models, such as Harvard, have also been closely analysed and imitated as Chinese (and other emerging nation) schools rapidly grow their MBA offerings.

5.2.1. Globalisation

Globalisation, and its many ramifications involving strategic alliances and linkages in global trade, is seen as an important and critical event for management education. An overarching theme within globalisation is that it has changed the character of the competitive dynamic within management education. However, it seems that the reach and effects of globalisation are contextually situated and, therefore, contingent for each region. Table 5.2 shows a summary of regional perspectives on globalisation.

Respondents stress the need to think beyond borders and understand the structure, functioning and culture of key economies around the world. The shift to the developing economies of the East (particularly China and India) and the South from developed Western economies provides options, and

Table 5.2: Perspectives on globalisation on a regional basis.

	EU	US	Asia
EU perspective on globalisation	International shifts within region built capacity and then global influence saw new market opportunities	Allows Europe to compete with US dominance; European identity and focus is seen as response to this	Opens new markets for students and supply of faculty although increasingly a competitor for both of these
US perspective on globalisation	'Not on the radar'; only impact was the advent of EQUIS, which has forced AACSB to become international	Globalisation is a source of new markets for management education, e.g. linkages with China, India, Latin America	Concern over the threat to US dominance from the emergence of leading European and Chinese schools
Asia perspective on globalisation	EU showed Asian universities that there was room for competitors	Leader and key competitor; initiates many of the ideas from leading US schools, e.g. Harvard	Strong emphasis on capacity building, e.g. rapid growth of Chinese MBA programmes and gaining global quality standing (via accreditations from AACSB and EQUIS)

opportunities, for the growth of management education in these regions. In essence, they see the strong emergence of China and India as very significant; and inexorable shift in the balance of power to Asia is resulting in a much more balanced emphasis on Asian as well as European and American viewpoints of management education. Some examples follow:

> The explosion of the global economy has required us to think beyond borders far more than we did. In 1990 we didn't think

across borders. There was no international perspective. It is now an overriding force. Now it has to be.

The next one is the whole issue of the opening up of the world: China, India, Singapore, South America, Africa ... globalisation. Opening up of a world away from a European/US-centric focus. I think that this was very important and it helped to pre-condition us for understanding the value of variety.

[The] emergence of a global playing field ... comes with rankings, agreements, specialised publications.

The emergence of China was important. [It] requires many business schools. China's changing policies on education [meant that] at one point they decided that they wanted to have a lot of MBAs, for people to get educated overseas, so they gave lots of exit visas and a whole bunch of Chinese nationals went overseas. China then decided they'd open some business schools — about 100 of them — and the exit visas all disappeared.

Another respondent identifies the important linkage between globalisation and technology and, particularly, the role of strategic alliances in the future evolution of management education. There is a sense, however, that the considerable potential of technology and strategic alliances has not yet been adequately exploited:

The future has got to have three things. It has to be global; it's got to stop being as American as it was. It's got to embrace technology and technology transfer. And finally it's going to have to work a lot more with alliances ... there have to be alliances because there is so much knowledge that is embedded in universities around the world and you have to use technology (and technology transfer) a lot more.

5.2.2. *Competition/Competitive Dynamics of Management Education (Including Privatisation)*

The landscape of competition in management education has been characterised by fast growth and intense rivalry. There have been a large number of publicly and privately funded entrants that have created a range of new MBA, EMBA and executive education programmes in response to the varied set of customer demands from businesses, governments and students.

The impact of the shift from academically oriented to more customer focused programmes is expressed in these comments:

> I think that today business schools have to be much more diversified then they were 20 years ago ... Schools, as well, have been adapting to working with companies in a much better way than they were 20 years ago.

> [Schools are now] more programme centric — schools are known because they have great MBA programmes or great Executive MBA programmes, etc. Nobody's known for having a great PhD programme. They may be, but perhaps just by a couple of people who are in the same discipline. The external environment has placed different sets of values on what make business schools good or better.

And the significance of EFMD's catalytic role in the growth of MBAs and business schools is also noted:

> The launch (by EFMD) of the Chinese business school CEIBS was a significant and audacious event.

And the decline in public funding for management education has forced many business schools to adopt privatisation strategies in order to raise operating revenue from high-tuition programmes (e.g. MBA, EMBA) and private endowment funding:

> Privatisation ... seems to be consistent worldwide. The traditional largely public sources of funding for higher education, including business education, are shrinking. Meaning that we have to rely more heavily on tuition and other forms of revenue and that's had a huge impact. It's had a huge impact not only on the diversity of our funding sources and the risks of our funding sources, but also had a huge impact on the culture of our business schools.

The use of privatisation strategies by more conventional business schools has brought them into close competition with the so-called 'for profit' business schools. One respondent speculates about the nature of this competition and the possibility that they will become commodity-type 'diploma mills':

> I think I was glad that the EFMD Board voted to let them ['for-profit' business schools] become members of the EFMD … we, the EFMD and the business schools are going to have to deal with this new way of looking at how a business school could be run. I worry about where the profits are going, that's my main concern. I'm not in favour of diploma mills but I am worried about that.

5.2.3. Emergence of a European Identity: European Competition in Management Education

In Chapter 3 we noted the comments of Nueno, Rameau and Borges on the importance of Europe to the competitive evolution of management education. Respondents expressed this in the following terms:

> I think 1990 saw a sea change in European business education where suddenly it wasn't a cottage industry in Europe but … part of a global, branding, competitive space and environment driven by a bunch of things, the obvious one is *Business Week* and *FT* rankings.

> I think that the next most important item was when EFMD decided that it was going to launch EQUIS because AACSB was just going to be domestic. It was going to be sleepy and it was going to be maybe quietly arrogant. When EFMD launched EQUIS, a number of people said 'holy smoke, maybe we'd better start going to the altar'. So I think that was very, very big because it was a wake-up call. At the time AACSB wasn't taking AMBA too seriously but I think that was because AMBA was focused on MBA programmes … when EQUIS came along and said that [it was] going to do it all, undergrad through PhD and going to add executive education … I think that woke up AACSB.

5.2.4. Accreditation and Professionalisation of the Sector

Accreditation is seen by European and emerging countries as a process that enhances the perception of their quality, image, globalisation and impact on management education. Various authors (e.g. Khurana, 2007) have seen accreditation processes and their associated quality standards as a vehicle for the professionalisation of management education:

> The development of EQUIS, which to me was basically the (European) business schools getting together and saying 'we don't want to go to the States — we'd rather be beaten on the head by Europeans than Americans. We'd rather do it ourselves' ... I think that changed management education and is still changing it dramatically.

> The other event is the push for international accreditation ... I think that AACSB decided to move beyond the US and Canada in the very late 1990s and the year 2000 did the pilot programmes ... the development of international accreditation was an influence.

An Asian respondent specifically addresses the value of reputation in enhancing the global profile and impact of a school:

> We already have EQUIS and we are working for AACSB — we are in the middle of the process. We did it because of consideration of more internationalisation and also to raise the impact globally.

A European respondent, however, stresses accreditation processes and quality assurance as part of the professionalisation of the management education industry:

> The importance of accreditation schemes in general (not specifically EFMD) is because they provide mechanisms and tools for quality assurance and quality improvement ... by definition, they are looking backwards. And I think that is the main one. It also has to do with the professionalisation of the industry — I think that there are always two sides to the coin. The other thing is the increasingly stronger voice from the corporate world in terms of what employers, recruiters and organisations expect from graduates.

5.2.5.   Rankings

Rankings are clearly seen to be significant as an expression of a new dynamic and a new competitive and consumer focus in management education:

> It is the emergence of rankings that has influenced heavily the way a lot of business schools think about their strategy.

I think that in the case specifically of our industry, business schools rankings, first in the US with *Business Week* and later on in the *Financial Times*, really can be considered an event that created new dynamics, at least for many schools that were used to seeing themselves in positions on only the domestic arena. Suddenly the rankings allowed those significant national players to compare themselves in the international arena, so that was a very significant event.

5.2.6. Exogenous Shocks

There are a number of exogenous shocks to management education that are consistently mentioned by respondents. These include financial and economic crises such as the 2008 global financial crisis and ethical failures involving companies such as ENRON and World Com.

We are grappling with all of these and I think that industry is dealing with these faster than we are, and we are playing catch up all the time in terms of what is that doing to our market, our customer base and our pedagogy.

Financial scandals such as ENRON and World Com panicked the business schools because the leaders of many of these organisations had MBAs. Many blamed the business schools, who had a strange response: 'We don't produce that many MBAs — not all of them do finance — you can't really blame us'.

There seems to be a key difference between respondents from different regions in how they view crises and corporate scandals. US/Canadian respondents do not appear to regard scandals such as ENRON as key events for the field whereas Europeans, Asian and South African respondents regard them as important in highlighting the need to study ethical issues in management education. They are also concerned about the reputational fallout for business schools from close association and imputed blame for these events.

On the other hand, US/Canadian respondents express much more concern about the impact of recession(s) on demand for management education whereas Asian, Europeans and South Africans are once again concerned with the lessons to be learned from them. They are continually troubled by the criticisms that business schools have been identified with by media commentators and educators. Consequently, business schools are seen as in some way complicit in training the architects of the most recent financial crisis.

5.2.7.   *Technology and Information*

Technology in its various forms — IT, Internet, digital/social media — is significant because it offers a series of options on delivery approaches for enhancing management education. However, there is a sense from most respondents that it has not yet reached its full potential:

> I think that the breakthrough of technology in the early 2000s has also been a trigger of change, probably one that has had less immediate impact than people assumed but probably has a bigger influence over the long term than what we see now.

Another respondent identified three impacts of technology in terms of programme delivery, student access to information and placement opportunities.

> The major event is technology. Opportunities opened up for jobs with companies like Yahoo and Google and for schools in terms of the ability (provided by technology) to deliver programmes. And students now have access to more information at their disposal — they can now get access to anything.

> [Technology is] not incremental in a linear way — the last four or five years with Facebook and all of these forms of social media have seen a significant rise … in this area. We are looking at many ways, as a school and as a university, of getting ourselves on to YouTube and iUniversity and all of these different forms of social media. That definitely wasn't the case 10 years ago.

Technology has clearly created a wide range of new options and opportunities. And as noted by one respondent the time factor and the speed of reaction to technology becomes important:

> The time factor has totally changed. You have to react within hours now, whereas in the past you could react within weeks. It has brought a major change to the competitive element because the information available to the people going to market is so much more extensive.

5.2.8. *Other Responses*

However, one respondent pointed out that the plea for a stronger corporate voice and presence in management education will become an increasingly important pressure point:

> The other event is the increasingly stronger voice from the corporate world in terms of what employers, what recruiter organisations expect from graduates … . Also we have a big communication issue with the corporate world … we may be doing relevant stuff but we are not telling the world, so it's not being translated or communicated.

And another points out this increased corporate pressure may not be successful because of the countervailing pressures on academics in business schools to produce high-quality academic research:

> My sense is that there is more pressure on being an academic: academics are more highly remunerated now in relative terms than they were. [However], expectations of their research productivity are higher and they're now under more pressure to deliver on that account. But that's only made them less relevant not more relevant to their principal stakeholders (students, businesses etc).

In summary, it is clear from interviewee responses that we are able to derive at least four competitive drivers from the macro-environment and two important facets of the management education sector from which key events originate (see Figure 5.1).

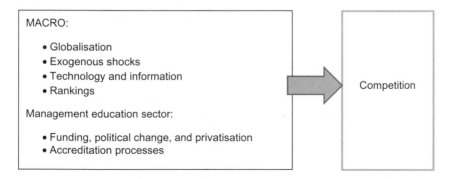

Figure 5.1: The competitive drivers in management education.

5.3. What Led to the Emergence of these Significant Events in Management Education?

A range of *external* drivers are behind the key events outlined above. Factors that led to the emergence of key events tend to belong to the macro-environment or the higher education sector. Indeed, many of the key events can be attributed to exogenous shocks and the effects of globalisation. The majority of respondents signalled that key events emerged from within higher education and the management education sector. Virtually the only example of internally generated key events is via 'visionary leaders' who put certain European schools on the map.

> We have had few very visionary leaders in business schools in Europe who had a clear vision and were able to implement that vision ... George Bain, for example, in his management of LBS ... Antonio Borges was also clearly a very strong leader for INSEAD.

> These have become leaders and also the templates for accreditors as, arguably, these early visionaries in Europe (and latterly Asia) set the standard for the top 20% of schools — '... the behaviour of the leading schools sets a pattern for the behaviour of others'.

This raises issues about the dynamics of the interaction between the role of business schools and management education in general. Business schools may perhaps be too passive and act in too reactive a manner in relation to their environment and in shaping management education:

> I would say that actually the greatest issues and impact have interestingly been exogenous. My conclusion from that is to go back to an earlier statement I made that business schools seem to seize the opportunities when they're there from exogenous events, such as government shifts and shifts in [economic activity] but actually they've had very little voice in shaping any of that. And I see them as reactive rather than proactive, and with a relatively small voice in some of the major shifts we have seen in the last 20 years.

Figure 5.2 demonstrates that the drivers of key events in management education are seen to occur at either the macro-environment or at the sector level. The following discussion explains why these drivers are seen as important to our respondents.

	Key event category	Key driver for ME	
MACRO	Globalisation	New markets, but increasingly, new competitors (e.g. Emergence of an European identity)	**Competition: Intensified competition for resources, students and faculty**
	Exogenous Shocks	Financial crises/recessions Significant social/political events Corporate scandals	
	Technology and Information	Role of social media and impact on reputation of schools New ways of teaching, learning and communicating with stakeholders	
	Rankings	Transparency. Legitimacy?	
ME Sector	Funding, Political Change and Privatisation	Combination of reduced government funding and deregulation of HE The arrival of for-profit schools.	
	Accreditation Processes	Professionalisation–heading towards a set of professional standards for ME, based on curricular and research quality. Has NOT resulted in the professionalisation of management. However, legitimacy for new or emerging schools has been achieved.	

Figure 5.2: The linkage between key events and key drivers in management education.

5.3.1. Globalisation

There is a clear view from our respondents that in the global environment the re-emergence of capitalism in some form or another (the re-unification of Germany, the collapse of the Soviet Union, the regeneration of China etc.) has signalled the end of Communism and, in turn, led to globalisation and global integration. Some comments from respondents reinforce this view:

> I think the underlying factor has been the trend towards more reliance on capitalism and markets [and] the integration of economies.

> Globalisation is not a policy decision … the driver(s) that underline this are complexity, internationalisation and the discontinuities brought about by the global system.

> The drivers have been technology and the influence of technologically driven communication. People know what happens in other countries and this has increased the demand levels.

With the emergence of global markets and globalisation business schools also recognised that their students needed global perspectives and insights about the way the world operates in their conduct of their rapidly developing global careers:

> Yes, the world is smaller. And corporations are indeed bigger [and] do need people who have a world view ... I think to have confident business managers in global corporations you have to have a world view.

5.3.2.   Exogenous Shocks

The observation that business schools tend to adopt a reactive stance in handling such issues as ethical scandals and financial crises is evident in the following comments:

> Enron was a different thing, wasn't it? Enron was that sort of MBA tarnish. I think that we saw many crooks with MBAs — and more recently, there was the wide perception that there were a whole lot of people who had effectively destroyed our economy who had MBAs. Well, you know, these people had other degrees as well. A lot of them had PhDs and you never actually in the normal scheme of things put a Masters degree above a PhD but somehow with an MBA you do.

> The financial crisis prompted the need for thought leadership. It is simply the bad part of human nature — the greed portion that said I want to get all I can for myself as fast as I can and to hell with everybody else. The issue is whether that was exacerbated in/by business schools.

5.3.3.   Technology and Information

Technology inspired by innovation, predominantly of US origin, is seen as an important driver of management education. It has been both an enabler of global markets in management education and a creator of strategic options for programme delivery in areas such as distance learning:

> For technology I think that we have to put it this way ... and this only happened about 15 years ago. Without the US, internet and the virtual world today would not be as it is. So people speak about the US decline but still the biggest

revolution over the last 15 years in terms of technology was originated, developed and commercialised in the US.

5.3.4.   *Funding, Political Change and Privatisation*

There are a range of alternative views about the influence of funding, politics and policy, and market-driven change. Policy change is, however, seen as an important factor:

> In the case of external factors I think it was policy and politics ... also the policy of opening trade to exporting countries mainly from emerging regions was very important for them and the whole world ... So I would say ... this actually highlights the importance of politics in society and the business world, the role of how you create and sustain the context for innovation, those are for me the important drivers.

From a funding viewpoint, it is clear that reductions in government funding are common:

> What I feel is that — and I am talking more about Europe than about the US — we need a parallel shift. Which is fine. Don't give support to education as you used to but then remove quickly all the impediments that will allow higher education institutions to make a living. Not only that, change the culture, allow schools and universities to differentiate themselves from the crowd.

And increasing demand patterns for management education drive market growth and, with reduced government funding, privatisation strategies:

> Why did the market grow? Probably because more and more people saw business education as a way for career development. At the undergraduate level it was very much a vocational degree that would lead to a job; at the postgraduate MBA level it was providing education that was going to be life transforming or career transforming. So I think that it was market driven.

5.3.5.   *Reputation of Management Education (Rankings and Accreditation)*

Rankings and accreditation are seen to be important drivers of a business school's reputation and image. Two viewpoints follow:

> I think that ranking and accreditation has to do with the value of reputation and the difficulty in measuring quality. So the best way to pull a school upwards is working on its reputation. But it is not necessarily the best from my point of view. It is probably, I would say, the easiest but that may not be … the way that is more likely to produce the right results.

> The emergence of rankings and accreditation is linked to globalisation. Rankings are differentiating elements and signalling devices.

In summary, the key drivers of competition are exhibited in Figure 5.3.

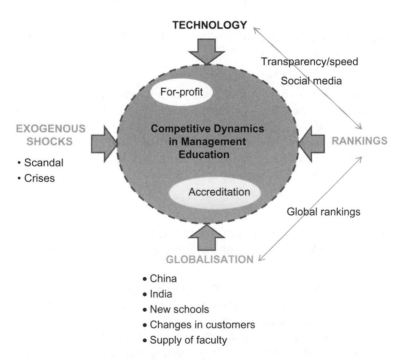

Figure 5.3: Competitive dynamics in management education: the key drivers of sustainable competitive advantage.

5.4. Summary and Conclusions

Following our review of the key events, it is important to identify the most important and significant events in management education over the last 20 years.

Having outlined the significant events and their key drivers we asked respondents to rank them in order of importance.

A total of 33 of the respondents ranked significant events giving a population of 85 nominations of significant events. This produced 39 unique events that have been sorted into 10 distinct categories (see Table 5.3).

It should be noted that the macro factors of globalisation, crises (exogenous shocks) and technology are seen as highly important. Rankings are not seen as quite as important. However, if rankings and accreditation processes are part of reputation management for business schools — a sector-level effect — then rankings become a very important element of the process of signalling image and reputation. In addition, at the sector level the role of policy and government was seen as much less significant.

5.5. Identifying the Most Significant Events

Twenty-seven of the respondents provided rating of the most significant event in management education (over the last 20 years) (see Table 5.4).

Table 5.3: The most important categories of events in management education.

Category	Number of times ranked (1st–5th)	Percentage of respondents ranking category 1st–5th (/33)	Percentage of all categories ranked (/85)
Globalisation	17	52	20
Accreditation	12	36	14
Crises	11	33	13
Political change	11	33	13
Technology	11	33	13
European identity	8	24	9
Rankings	7	21	8
Competition	4	12	5
MBA/Exec Ed	3	9	4
Environment	1	3	1

Table 5.4: The most significant event in management education.

Most significant event	Percentage of respondents
Technology	19
Accreditation/AACSB/EQUIS	18
Globalisation	11
Passport to wealth	4
Government funding	4
Bologna	4
Thatcherism	4
Government policy	4
All	4
Growth of the MBA	4
Innovation and programme growth	4
Ethics crisis	4
Academic salaries	4
Rankings	4
Exogenous events	4
9/11	4
Financial crisis	4
Total	

Technology is most frequently cited by respondents as the most significant event in management education. This is attributed to technology's capacity as an 'enabler' — technology has been a key driver in globalisation, helping to underscore the impact of business school rankings (transparency), and pushes innovation in programme development and growth. Therefore, technology and globalisation are seen as interlinked since the acceleration of global competition and global business are driven largely by the possibilities provided by IT. Further, accreditation and rankings are also rated as most significant, indicating that they jointly feature in establishing the reputation and image of business schools.

Chapter 6

Opinion Leaders, Distinctly Different Schools and Innovations in Management Education

6.1. Introduction

Much has changed in management education in the 15 years since the EFMD published the '*Training The Fire Brigade*', a volume celebrating EFMD's 25th anniversary. Significant events such as globalisation, advances in information technology, continued growth in the market and student numbers, the prominence and expansion of accreditation bodies, and an increasing focus on rankings are all driving changes in the relationships and influence of stakeholders in management education.

Both rankings and accreditation agencies are seen as among the most significant internal influences on the management education sector. Many business school deans and university administrators view rankings as an increasingly important signal of reputation. However, it is not only business, faculty and students that have influenced the conduct of management education over the last 20 years. We asked interviewees to consider which individuals and organisations have been most influential, becoming opinion leaders in the field. In total, this question provided a list of 56 influential individuals and the Top 10 most frequently nominated influential individuals are shown in Table 6.1.

6.1.1. Which Individuals Have Had the Greatest Influence on Management Education?

The most frequently nominated opinion leaders in management are Henry Mintzberg and Peter Drucker. From a total of 39 respondents the population of 56 opinion leaders indicates inconsistent (or perhaps regional/localised)

Table 6.1: Opinion leaders in management education — individuals.

Leaders	Mentions	Era active	Role/Position	Dean/Head of school (Yes (Y), No (N))
Peter Drucker	13		Guru	N
Henry Mintzberg	13		Guru/Academic	N
C.K. Prahalad	6		Academic	N
Michael Porter	6		Academic	N
Peter Lorange	5		Academic/ Entrepreneur	Y
George Bain	4		Academic	Y
Charles Handy	3		Philosophy of management education	N
Sumantra Ghoshal	3		Academic	N
Herbert Simon	3		Academic	N
Jim March	3		Academic	N

perceptions of who has had an influence on management education. It is remarkable that only two (gurus) stand out as opinion leaders and no deans other than Peter Lorange (IMD, Lorange Institute) and George Bain (LBS) receive any mention at all. Their contributions are identified in our later discussion of distinctly different schools. In many respects both of them fall in the category of visionary management education leaders.

The respondents' viewpoints about individuals are clearly indicated in the following quotations. Others note that writers such as Charles Handy and Sumantra Ghoshal (2005) have focused on what is wrong with business schools, particularly on the role of liberal education in management schools and also emphasise the value of real-world learning in the classroom. Jim March and Herb Simon (1958) wrote the definitive material on organisational behaviour and organisational decision processes in management education.

> Drucker, Porter, Prahalad have shaped the way that business schools have thought about being a business school. They have also influenced the way managers of large organisations have thought about what it is that they do.

Visionary people: usually those who contribute something to the field. So academics: Drucker, Prahalad, Chandler and people like that. I don't think that people are interested in the kind of visionaries who lead schools.

I think Charles Handy in the UK for a while did some really innovative thinking although I think that some of his subsequent books tended to be a re-statement, a bit like Peter Drucker, whose earliest work was actually the most interesting.

Henry Mintzberg has always attracted attention as a strident critic of the process and content of management education.

Some have been bluntly critical, like Mintzberg, and others have been more diplomatically critical, like Lorange in Europe, to give you an example of someone who is closer to us ... I think that the two of them have contributed because they have provided some shaking, which sparks critical thinking and which forces us to look at ourselves. I am not sure that in the end all these initiatives have a drastic impact but I do think that they have had an evolutionary impact; they have raised concern about certain aspects and people have taken them more seriously.

I'm thinking of rogue academics — Mintzberg had enormous influence. He hasn't always come across well nor all of what he has said has necessarily been accepted, but I think that a lot of what he's done is 'spot on'.

I think that the other people who then came through were, for me, less involved with fads and fashions and movements in academia but people like Mintzberg, who I rarely agree with, actually had an impact on the field in a way I think quite remarkable and is probably akin to Michael Porter. It's remarkable because not only did those two people have an influence on academic research but they were also eulogised by students. You can read any MBA or masters student's essay from Mannheim to Bologna and you will find Porter and Mintzberg mentioned.

A distinguishing feature of all these individuals is their emphasis on management as a practice and their consequent attraction for aspiring leaders. Indeed, Mintzberg, Drucker, Prahalad and Porter have dominated 'Thinkers 50' — a global ranking of management thinkers published by business school critics Stuart Crainer and Des Dearlove (1998) — since the rankings began in 2001. Drucker was voted top management thinker in 2001 and 2003, Porter in 2005 and Prahalad in 2007 and 2009, underlining their influence on management thought inside and outside management education.

Porter and Prahalad have dominated the practice of competitive strategy. Porter's five forces model of industry competition and Prahalad's discussions of the strategic intent and the core competences at the firm level have strongly influenced analytic models of strategy.

For Drucker, management is an integrated practice — an art of balancing *managing a business*, *managing managers* and *managing worker and work*. With management practice in mind, Mintzberg holds a mirror up to management education in his book *Managers not MBAs* (2004), which is scathing of the skills taught in management education, not to mention its damaging effect on the quality of management. The birth of management schools, leading to a set of core (and competing) disciplines and analytical approaches, means that they are often ill equipped to deliver integrated management education that resembles the skills that Drucker and Mintzberg identify as essential. What we can conclude from this is that management practice requires a holistic and integrated set of skills. However, management education is best structured to deliver teaching in discipline-oriented silos leaving students with a distorted view of management and the immense task of integrating their own learning.

Another individual in the Top 5, Peter Lorange, has also had a direct impact on management education through his initiatives as dean of IMD, the creation of an innovative learning model and the establishment of the Lorange Institute of Business in Switzerland. These individuals stand out because we have not yet worked out how to teach the kind of management they describe. Alongside influential individuals are the schools and organisations that deliver management education, we asked respondents to identify which schools have influenced management education.

6.1.2. *Which Business Schools or Organisations Have Had the Greatest Influence on Management Education?*

In terms of leading organisations, 36 respondents identified 42 different organisations they considered opinion leaders in management education — those with two or more mentions appear in Table 6.2. It appears that the

Table 6.2: Opinion leaders in management education — organisations.

Leading organisation	Mentions
EFMD/EQUIS	14
AACSB	9
Business Week	3
FT (*Financial Times*)	3
Harvard	3
INSEAD	2
Carnegie Mellon	2
Leading US schools	2
Government	2

trade/professional and accreditation bodies hold a dominant position. These are followed by the two major business school rankings, those in the *FT* and *Business Week*. Leading US business schools, Harvard and Carnegie Mellon are the third most important opinion leaders. INSEAD and governments also appear in the opinion leaders.

Accreditation bodies and rankings receive nearly three-quarters of all mentions. This attests to their significance in building reputation and assuring quality in business schools.

> The role of EFMD is also important because it acted as a home, an influence and as a nurturer for those accredited, to help disparate scholars, often working in small departments in large universities, where their voice wasn't heard, their research wasn't published. So I think that those have been important.

Government has some limited influence, and impact, on management education:

> National governments, if you think about the US government and in Europe, perhaps more than national governments the European Union, are actually helping promote some initiatives, infrastructure and technology. Those are very important drivers of change in different ways. In addition, the development of the internet and projects within the defence department in the US raised technology knowledge. So at a government level, I think this is important.

And, some of the US business schools, particularly Harvard, have had a consistently strong influence:

> Harvard, but its insistence on, I was going to say moral superiority but let's say academic superiority and commitment, rightly or wrongly, to excellence, had a huge influence on other schools. These US schools ... were very influential in the globalisation of management education.

> I think that Harvard is still very, very strong. The amazing thing is Harvard in China, on a scale of 1 to 10 scores 10. And the second-best scores about 3, although they are also very good. But the tremendous pulling power in China is Harvard. And I do think they are still very impressive. I think ... they have managed to become a reference for many other business schools, including those who actually are enormously different from them.

However, despite the growing significance of accreditation agencies in gaining recognition for business schools, some of our respondents believe that their influence on management education is not very great.

> If I may put it this way — and this is a comment that comes from a sense of admiration for the work they do but also a realisation that perhaps the work they do does not have a bigger impact ... AACSB and EFMD do a lot of things but I am afraid that they used to have more impact 20 years ago than they have today in terms of how business schools actually think. So I am afraid that they are several steps behind some of the challenges ... Business schools and management education have to choose much more dynamism, ... When I go to the SMS conference or the Academy of Management meetings there are many interesting ideas, more so than when I go to an EFMD conference, at least that's my feeling.

6.1.3.   Which Business Schools Are Distinctly Different?

We asked more specifically which business schools have achieved clear distinction and differentiation.

Table 6.3 is drawn from 36 interviewees. In total they nominated 46 institutions as being distinctly different. Table 6.3 shows only those

Table 6.3: Distinctly different providers of management education.

Institution	Mentions	Country/Region	University/Independent
IMD	16	Europe	Independent
INSEAD	11	Europe	Independent
Harvard	9	US/North America	University
WBS	6	UK/Europe	University
LBS	6	UK/Europe	Independent
Wharton	5	US/North America	University
CEIBS	5	China/Asia	Independent
Cranfield	4	UK/Europe	University
Open University	4	UK/Europe	University
None	4		
MIT	4	US/North America	University
Ashridge	4	UK/Europe	Independent
Chicago Booth	3	US/North America	University
Stanford	3	US/North America	University
IESE	3	Spain/EU	University
Melbourne	2	Aus/NZ	University
SAID	2	UK/Europe	University
Dartmouth	2	US/North America	University
HKUST	2	HK/Asia	University
Lancaster	2	UK/Europe	University
Aalto	2	Scandinavia	University
Lyon	2	France/Europe	Independent
Phoenix	2	US/North America	For-profit

institutions that received more than one nomination from our interviews. IMD, INSEAD and Harvard emerge as dominant institutions.

Insights about IMD, INSEAD and LBS can be gleaned from a recently completed extensive research study (Fragueiro & Thomas, 2011) of the leadership processes in five leading schools: IAE, IMD, INSEAD, LBS and WBS. In the case of IMD (founded 1992/1993), INSEAD (founded 1960s) and LBS (founded 1965/1966), they examined their internationalising processes in the period 1990–2004 when these schools transformed from being very strong European schools into excellent, internationally competitive business schools consistently ranked in the top 10–15 of the *Financial Times* Ranking of Global MBA Programmes.

The role of strong deans, who had the time and courage to implement their visioning and positioning strategies, is evident in the actions of such as Bain at LBS, Borges, de Meyer and Hawawini at INSEAD and Lorange at

IMD. Bain faced the challenge of strategic transformation of LBS from a well-known UK school to an international school. He used his strong reputation as a change agent to set a clear strategic change agenda. Borges promoted and strategised the growth of INSEAD as a leading research school and a business school for the world with an overseas campus in Singapore. Lorange shaped IMD's strategy of simplicity with four elements: 'Real life, real learning', 'The global meeting place', 'All learning is lifelong learning', and 'A minimalist organisational approach'. He is further applying his newer model of the networked business school at his own school, the Lorange Institute of Business in Zurich.

In this internationalising process each of these schools built up strong reputational and stakeholder capital that led to a very significant level of recognition by other business schools, business leaders, media and professional organisations. Similarly, over 100 years HBS has reinforced its strong pioneering reputation and image as a leading business school. It is regarded very highly internationally for its pedagogical innovations including case studies and many textbooks, the influence of the *Harvard Business Review* and Harvard Business School Press books and the continuing high quality of HBS faculty. They have also reinforced these advantages through consistently stable leadership and a financial endowment that enables them to maintain strong investments in faculty and innovative management education.

It is no surprise, therefore, to see Harvard, INSEAD, IMD and LBS identified as strong influencers in management education. It should be noted that they are all essentially private universities and in the case of IMD, INSEAD and LBS 'stand-alone' business schools. WBS (founded 1967), on the other hand, is an example of a publicly funded, university-based business school that managed to grow innovatively (e.g. with the construction of an extremely well-regarded blended distance learning MBA programme) and gained a strong reputation in the context of an entrepreneurial university through the strong initial leadership of Bain and more recently Thomas (2000–2010).

Other schools occupy niche positions in the field. For example Cranfield is known for its work on entrepreneurship, a practical MBA and executive education programmes while The Open University has developed a unique blended learning platform for distance learning MBAs. With EFMD sponsorship CEIBS has also created a very strong position as a leading Asian (Chinese) MBA school. And Wharton, MIT and Chicago are highly rated pioneer US business schools whereas Stanford is known as the 'Harvard of the West' and as an innovative West Coast school.

What does it mean to be different? Respondents see this in terms of regional differences (which affect the character of management education, e.g. Antunes & Thomas, 2007) and in terms of the relationship, if any, with their university institution, particularly, physics envy and legitimacy (Thomas & Wilson, 2011).

If it comes to the general things, I feel that, as a European businessman, that a European or Asian business school has more to offer than the American one ... We all know that American business schools are very good but I think that they are still too inward looking ...

I think a lot of our business schools would be a darn sight better off if they were in a similar relationship with their institutions — particularly the ancient institutions. The business schools inside the Edinburghs and Durhams really struggle and a lot of it is to do with institutional norms and these old-fashioned establishments, which are very centralised.

6.1.4. What Have Been the Major Innovations in Management Education Over the Last 20 Years?

We also asked our respondents to name what they see as the major innovations in management education over the last 20 years. The most commonly cited innovation is the influence of information technology, especially its role in delivering distance and e-learning. However, precisely what impact IT-driven innovation has had on management education is a contested issue. This varies according to respondents' accounts of the pace and scale of change; most report a step change in IT (radical innovation) compared with others who argue that the role of technology has involved more cautious developments (impact of IT-driven innovation) (Table 6.4).

A second area of innovation in management education occurs in the content and delivery of management courses. The growth of distance learning courses (worldwide) is seen as intertwined with innovation in technology as well as innovations in scalable forms of teaching and assessment for management students. Respondents identify sources of change (some are reluctant to use the term 'innovation') in the following areas in management education:

(1) *Subject areas in management education*
   There have been some incremental improvements in management education curricula such as CSR and entrepreneurship but the impression is that they are viewed as faddish.
   There is a clear sense that there have been few, or more likely no, radical changes in curricula. However, there is evidence of a current push towards integrated, holistic curricula
   • 'There have been the kinds of incremental improvements that have allowed us to understand the nature of management itself. So there

Table 6.4: Impact of IT-driven innovation.

Incremental change from IT	Radical change from IT
… we fine-tuned our use of technology in the classroom and our understanding and appreciation of it is much better, but do I see anyone who's been totally revolutionary with technology and pedagogy — I don't think so.	… if I look at things that are salient, the use of e-learning is probably more revolutionary, more different from what happened years ago. Well there is obviously the whole area that has to do with technology. It changes the way we live, interact and communicate, in the broader sense, so it also has an effect on how people learn. Technology — the way we deliver the curriculum. Don't think that we have even reached the limit on that — everything is electronic-assignments handed in electronically, can grade things by voice, etc. —we never have to touch a piece of paper. We can give people much better feedback this way than by just giving notes. Technology — computers, personal response devices, e-delivery — can engage classes in ways you could not before and facing classes of 500 you can do it. New material and forms of delivery.

have been some disparate improvements. But I don't think that they're paradigm shifting … Nor has there been a radical change in curriculum.'

- 'Innovation in subject areas, for example in entrepreneurship and CSR has come through strongly recently. Some of those I see as faddish, although not entrepreneurship. [There have also been] developments in subject areas such as finance but I don't necessarily see those as innovation.'
- 'Ten or 15 years ago, the most popular courses tended to be [things like] Finance for Non-Financial Managers, the functional type of courses. I think a fundamental innovation today is more and more programmes that are cross-disciplinary, multi-functional and integrative rather than highly specialised programmes.'

(2) *Globalisation*

While globalisation is seen as a significant influence in management education its promise is yet to be fully achieved. Student exchanges are now common but more needs to be done to bring global, cultural knowledge and intelligence into the curricula

- 'I suppose we can say that there is more a change in terms of internationalisation, where you have had more students and faculty coming from different countries.'
- 'Business schools, especially in Europe, have been quite good at adjusting to globalisation. I think that this is a very important innovation from being very much Europe-centric ... As for US schools, they still have a long way to go. Asian schools are already developing a lot but I think that from a management viewpoint this is an important achievement because you look at other higher education institutions and you don't see any other type of institution that has been so successful in terms of adjusting.'

(3) *Role of faculty*

Faculty's role is seen to be changing. Programme innovations require greater flexibility in faculty teaching assignments and a greater awareness of balancing teaching and research excellence

- 'Switched from a model where there used to be a faculty person and they are the curricula (German model) to a system where we can take faculty and create scale economies by plugging them into the curriculum to create specialists. Used to be that faculty time was based on the courses they teach; we would give them an assignment, now people are given multiple assignments. They have multiple responsibilities they have to deal with.'
- 'I always think of the kid in China taking a programme done by an English-speaking faculty member, the fact that it's supported by technology, that they can rewind it and review it, they have a much better chance of getting it than the old way, where we take really good notes and try to internalise those and then the class has gone.'

(4) *Competition and performance*

The arrival of 'for-profits' and privatisation of business schools has changed the competitive dynamics in the business school industry. Many business schools are questioning the sustainability of existing business models by adjusting not only their programme portfolios but also the faculty cost balance between tenure track and clinical faculty

- 'The arrival of the for-profits, who are trying to disaggregate our industry, like other competitors trying to disaggregate other traditional state-owned monopoly like picking off low-cost airlines, trying to stick it to BA, or personal services like the post office, etc.'
- 'I [also] think that we have to offer state-of-the art facilities, especially if want to compete for executive education and that sort of

thing ... We are concerned now about rankings and league placements and it maybe goes hand in hand with having a smart building and technology.'

- 'People talk a lot about competition from the for-profit sector but they talk less about how business schools have become better at profit seeking ... I think that there has been a fair amount of innovation in their ability to seek profits, despite their not-for-profit purpose.'

No one interviewed suggested that there have been any 'game-changing' innovations within management education. In this sense, it still resembles its former self in spite of dramatic changes in technology, economies, globalisation and business scandals. There is a high degree of stability in the system, which seems remarkably resilient to exogenous shocks.

There is also some internal criticism of developments in management education:

> AACSB should have been able to control the low end of the industry and it is a mistake not to have done this. Now these (low-end) guys have 10,000 students with an MBA and, if you believe in the statistics they told me, the top 1% of the 10,000 guys who have the MBA will probably be the reservoir of the entrepreneurs of tomorrow. And maybe in this top 1%, simply by a statistical thing, you have super-bright [people] ... And in all the newspapers it will be written that this new entrepreneur has a degree from the University of Phoenix. And for the next article, two pages later on in the same newspaper it will be saying another financial institution came down in the east coast and of course it's again a guy from Harvard (or a leading business school) involved, that he is a crook from Bank So and So, and this creates a 'biased' perspective on competition.

6.2. Summary and Conclusions

The most influential opinion leaders have not been deans but academics/ academic philosophers such as Drucker, Mintzberg and Handy who have seriously questioned whether management schools educate managers in a practical, holistic, liberal manner.

Academic gurus such as Porter and Prahalad have addressed and translated strategic issues such as competition and strategic execution in a readable manner. And all of them, without exception, have bridged the gap between academic research and managerial relevance and provided strong appeal to leaders, managers and business school participants.

Similarly, the most influential organisations — the accreditation agencies and rankings providers — have enabled business schools to build their external reputations. And the most distinctive and differentiated business schools are mainly the European leaders (IESE, IMD, INSEAD, LBS) and the US leaders (Chicago Harvard, MIT, Stanford, Wharton). Niche players such as Cranfield, OUBS and CEIBS are, in turn, admired for their distinctive niches and segment foci, respectively in entrepreneurship, CSR, blended learning and a strong China-focused MBA.

Finally, and sadly perhaps, there is a clear perception that, as yet, there have been no 'game-changing' innovations in management education. There is, therefore, a clear space for innovating and hence building distinctiveness around innovation in the future.

Chapter 7

The Main Issues in Management Education: What Are the Lessons Learned and Not Learned from the Past?

7.1. Introduction

In this chapter we first examine the most important issues in management education identified by our respondents and then draw on this background to identify the lessons that can be learned from the past and those that appear not to have been learned.

7.2. The Main Issues in Management Education

Table 7.1 shows a frequency table of the main issues. Certain key themes recur: globalisation, the gap between theory development and management practice in management education, changing competition and market growth worldwide, and, finally, continued questioning of the content of curricula (i.e. what management is about).

Table 7.2 shows responses in terms of the main stakeholder groups in our sample, which gives an interesting indication of the degree of consensus about the leading issues within stakeholder groups.

A quick summary of the responses from the alternative stakeholder perspectives suggests the following initial observations:

- First, a variety of issues are considered 'main' issues.
- Second, these range from internal characteristics of the industry to external shocks and threats.
- Third, there is little consensus in businesses/private sector about what the main issues facing management education are.

Table 7.1: Top issues identified across *all* respondents.

Issue	% of all mentions
Globalisation	26
Theory/Practice gap	18
Competition	18
Growth of management education	18
Curricula	18
Financial sustainability	12
Role of research	12
Rankings	12

Table 7.2: Top issues identified across by stakeholder groups.

Issue	% of all mentions
Academics	
Globalisation	35
Growth of management education	24
Silos	18
Technology	18
Competition	18
Relationship with university	12
Theory/Practice gap	12
Role of research	12
Environmental sustainability	12
Financial sustainability	12
Rankings	12
Faculty	6
Decline in state finding	6
Fads	6
Media	6
US/EU research	6
Scandal	6
Lack of change	6
Media	
Rankings	67
Scandal	33
Curriculum	33
Theory/Practice gap	33

Table 7.2: (*Continued*)

Issue	% of all mentions
Growth of management education	33
Role of business schools	33
Trade associations	
Globalisation	44
Competition	33
Curriculum	33
Role of research	22
Theory/Practice gap	22
Lack of change	11
Ethics	11
Management skills	11
Reactionary	11
Financial sustainability	11
Faculty	11
Individualisation	11
Accreditation	11
Growth of management education	11
Businesses/Private sector	
CLIP	20
Scandal	20
Need to look to the future	20
EQUIS	20
Silos	20
Financial sustainability	20
Curriculum	20

- Fourth, concerns over curricula (relevance, currency, providing skills for managers) are raised by all stakeholders except, very surprisingly, academics!
- Fifth, globalisation is the top issue for academics and trade associations.
- Finally, the financial stability of the business school model is mentioned by all groups apart from the media.

The more detailed comments on these issues are illustrated in the following quotations.

7.2.1.   Globalisation

Globalisation resonates through many of the responses to this question. However, few respondents articulate further *why* it is that globalisation (or internationalisation) is a main issue for management education except to indicate that globalisation has encouraged a degree of experimentation and innovation in business schools. These are some of the more developed responses:

> The growth of internationalisation in most of the leading business schools has been one of the key issues in this period. It has been the period where I think we have seen more schools betting on this. And I think that it was a good choice.

> Changing emphasis [to] more global [is a] key driver. Doesn't mean that you have to have a department of international business but you have to think about that — relevant curriculum, make students aware of globalisation, do things to enhance that ability, get them to go overseas. And the faculty have to do it too — [you] can't be a global institution and the faculty never go anywhere. [They] need to do sabbaticals, be engaged in the global marketplace. Whether a small or large business school, in a large metropolitan area or not, you have to participate. Business schools are now closer as a community because of globalisation. [They have] become more aware of the existence and emergence of other institutions, with innovative programmes operating everywhere in the world. [As a result] the competitive factor becomes stronger.

> [Globalisation] started around the 1990s so [we began] expanding the geographical scope of our programmes, alliances with other schools, change programmes for the MBA programme. So globalisation has clearly had an impact. And ... not just in terms of strategic moves but also in terms of how you actually include more international content in the programmes.

7.2.2.   Relationship with Universities

Respondents pick up on two dynamics in this important relationship. First is 'physics envy' (business schools' desire to emulate the scientific rigour of the sciences in business research) and the role of business schools within universities. Second, schools outside universities have experienced a drive to conduct rigorous research in order to compete, though a European respondent argues that some of those leading European schools are well positioned to make a more relevant contribution to management education simply because of their positioning outside universities:

> The role of the business school within universities [and] the relationship with the university can be a very difficult one. I think that is a major issue ... it is always an issue of about how you define the role between what is a professional school and the rest of the university.

> Many of the business schools, not just in Spain but also in France and in other places, were to a large extent outside the university system. But as research has become a much more a core element of the strategy and business model of the leading business schools across Europe, [we now have similar controversy as the US] as to whether we need to rebalance the role of research or at least the type of research that is carried out by faculty members. I think that European business schools are in a good position to offer a kind of middle ground as we are much more engaged in executive education. If we do it properly we can really benefit a lot from that.

> I think that we know how to think about the problem and what's required but I fear that we aren't able to deliver it because we are stuck in a world of universities where the incentives and rewards are not in line with what we want.

7.2.3. Role of Research

As noted in the discussion of the Business 2.0 developments in Chapter 2, it was clearly the advent of the Gordon/Howell reports in the late1950s that created the requirement for rigorous research in business schools.

> Twenty years ago ... research in management was basically non-existent and in many cases even judged to be irrelevant. One of the issues has been ... to do what the Ford Foundation argued in the 1950s — that is, you have to give a much stronger research base to what you teach. And while that

happened in the States much earlier than it happened in Europe, I think that is now a settled issue.

I think that we have seen in this period is a consolidation of and value of proper academic education on the part of faculty. Which I think is good because it brings some rigour to the thinking in management. But at the same time the evil is that we have transformed this to thoughtless publish or perish endeavour. But then again there is something good in moving from schools where things were too excessively theoretical to schools where they were excessively pragmatic without some rationalisation about what was going on in management education.

The problem about research [is] the huge demands both from academia itself and for the process of promotion in academia, particularly in the US for publishing in "good" journals, partly to emulate what goes on in more academic subjects. But against that there's this feeling that there's a lot of rubbish out there, which even though it may be intellectually interesting, doesn't actually do anything.

I've been very frustrated about the unquestioned assumption that having a PhD in a good subject and publishing in good journals is a necessary and sufficient condition to be a good teacher. And that seems to be totally un-provable and probably wrong. We need to concentrate much more on what is good teaching and what is good research. So I think that that tension between research and the practice of teaching continues to be a big problem.

7.2.4. Disciplinary Silos

Research is also found mainly in the sub-disciplines of business. Unfortunately there is no evidence of broad multi-disciplinary perspectives in business school research.

When I left Harvard and went to MIT, a lot of the thinking there at that time was inspired by Carnegie Tech and we talked a lot and practised a lot about team work, co-teaching, co-research, even to the point that the dean strongly favoured team-oriented articles. Amazing. We were doing teamwork with aeronautics, mathematics even. The whole thing was a team-sized project. … We all said that it was going so well we started to scale up the place from 45 to 80 and it all collapsed. Then we ended up with silos and we didn't know each other.

[There has been] a failure to engage in Big Picture Debates on management education and too much fragmentation and the silos are too narrow. This is still a problem. We are not looking at management education broadly enough.

7.2.5. Scandals

It is argued that the existence of corporate scandals and financial crises creates an important focus on what should be the purpose of management education in society.

There has been an important introspection about the role and function of business education and I think that that has been specifically post the 2007 financial crisis. And there was a whole lot of breast-beating about oh my God, are we teaching people the right stuff, have we caused this. I think there was a similar amount of breast-beating in the 1999–2000 range with some of the Enron etc bad corporate behaviour. So I think that has usefully thrown back into focus the question of what is the function of business within a society [and], therefore, what is the function of management education?

If you think about the response to the current crisis, we couldn't stand aside from that and say it's nothing to do with us. It could be said that it was to do with perverse incentives. However, I wonder whether the image that a lot of management educators have is that companies live in the land of plenty and have become divorced from the reality of CSR, value systems and so on. Perhaps now it has gone the other way and people are thinking that CSR should be embedded into the curriculum, people should be made much more aware of issues of giving back rather than taking.

7.2.6.   *Growth of Management Education*

However, over the last 20 years management education has grown faster and in a more successful manner than any other subject in modern universities, sometimes without adequate quality control:

> Management education has become very popular — it's the biggest major in the world — and managing that volume of students without a model of developing capable faculty is a big problem. We have a report in 2003 about sustaining scholarship in business schools that says that you need to have a strong cadre, i.e. sufficient numbers, of academically qualified faculty in order for the model to be sufficiently scalable in a global context. We need a global model for developing faculty that everybody has to go through before they are allowed at least to teach university students. It's not a very well controlled environment where you've got lots of start-ups that are just trying to make money from business education. Big problem!

7.2.6.1.   Growth in China

> The first nine programmes, in that first year in 1991, only enrolled 94 people. But in 2010, we had 236 MBA programmes and the student enrolment number is around 37,000.

> Growth — and especially faculty growth — is a bit easier now than 10 or 15 years ago. I think that the appeal of some European schools has brought some faculty from the US job market, so this has been important.

7.2.6.2.   With Growth Comes Competition

> I think that the last 20 years have been particularly noteworthy because the markets for what business schools produce have generally been burgeoning and at the same time, the group of providers or suppliers has expanded considerably as well. So the main trend has been a situation that is both attractive in terms of its ability to achieve greater resourcing but also competitive in the sense that it's attractive, or there are various markets that are attractive for others.

7.2.7. *Competition*

Global growth means that competitors with alternative management education models have emerged and challenged existing models of provision:

> A lot of [corporate universities] have succeeded, although a lot of them haven't, though they're still there. I think that from when they started to now, business schools can now live with corporate universities. There's a much better relationship between the two than when they started out.

> Business schools are now closer as a community because of globalisation. [They have become] more aware of the existence and emergence of other institutions with innovative programmes operating everywhere in the world.

7.2.8. *Curriculum*

In turn, this has resulted in a more thorough and critical examination of the management education curriculum:

> The realisation that the initial move into management education (talking mainly about the US) in the 1960s and 1970s was towards making it a mathematical subject, with an emphasis on statistics, mathematical formulae etc, managing a company by its financials. [It] didn't work .... Well, it worked to some extent but it somehow broke down in the overall motto that MBA students couldn't manage people and this became a mantra. This had to result in much more emphasis on leadership, soft skills, etc.

7.2.9. *Theory/Practice and the Role of Business Schools*

The debate concerning the worth of an MBA has stimulated debate about the value proposition of the business school itself. Is it about teaching the process of management or explaining a set of tools and techniques?

> People are still looking for tools from management education, rather than education.

Subjects such as ethics, sustainability etc. come and go — I wouldn't say that that is one of the main issues.

Business schools never defined what management education is, i.e. what is a manager, what does managing involve and so on. There's a lot in the leadership literature but I think that management education took a bit of a wrong turn with the emphasis on data collection when it really is about managing people.

Management as a practice is not examined. [There is] too much focus by academics on narrow problems using arcane mathematical techniques. But practical management has a status problem — too many over-simplified airport books that ignore the big picture and the complexity of management.

The urge to develop management as a science [with the quality and attributes of scientific work] and the desire to transform management schools to produce more PhD programmes ha[ve] exacerbated the tension between the professional and academic sides.

7.2.10.   *Rankings*

The media have largely created rankings. They have generated criticism and concern because they motivate schools to focus on areas that enhance the image and reputation of a school to the probable detriment of innovation and quality processes in management education:

Business schools have a love/hate affair with rankings and what to do about them.

Business schools jockeying for status and power because of league tables, rankings, etc. is anathema to others in an educational context. I do think that EFMD [with] EQUIS, as pioneers, saw accreditation as something that helped raise the quality. But it has also contributed to this jockeying for position and power and exclusivity and [it] may have to think again about touching base with helping and supporting.

7.3.   What Led to Their Emergence as Key Issues?

We then examined these issues and asked respondents what they considered to be the main forces driving the emergence of these issues, which are shown in Tables 7.3–7.9.

Table 7.3: Globalisation as a key issue.

Globalisation	Business happens in a smaller world and many nations are now involved. We train managers far beyond our own borders and the reach of the business school is now much further than its home base.
	The mobility of students and faculty has reshaped management education.
	Technology has made the world a smaller place to do business. As a consequence, competition within management education now operates globally (beyond its national base)
	There is now demand for 'international managers' on international courses.
	Globalisation is the overarching driver of demand for management education and the growth of business schools.
	First, it is fuelled by market circumstances — rapid growth and emerging economies. For management education globalisation has created herd behaviour; a perceived pressure to go international is felt and schools do not want to be left behind. There is a sense of short-termism and no overall strategy underlying the internationalisation of management education.

Table 7.4: Theory/Practice as a key issue.

Theory/ Practice and the role of research	Without academic thinking management education could not have joined higher education. However, this hasn't helped the practising manager.
	Ford/Carnegie reports created a push for academic legitimacy in business schools.

Table 7.4: (*Continued*)

The Carnegie report pushed for academic rigour (in the US) although it is hard to argue that the world is better managed because of the push for academic research.

At the point of becoming part of universities there are questions about the role of business schools in generating and transferring knowledge — the push for research has seen pedagogy and teaching take a secondary role to research.

A focus on A-journals has become a focus on arcane journals with no impact. Citations do not equate to impact; they are academic currency. The focus on A-journals impedes debate.

Academic currency is irrelevant (to management practice) research — therefore there is little, if any, impact on practice from management research.

The search (and pressure) for academic legitimacy is intense; however, management is seen as a minor intellectual player.

Table 7.5: Competition within management education as a key issue.

Competition	Globalisation — the mobility of labour, capital, technology and information — in combination with a general decline in government funding for higher education has heightened competition in management education. The arrival of for-profit providers has intensified competition for students.
	The fact that competition within management education now operates beyond borders has redefined how schools compete.
	Customer voice is becoming an increasingly important competitive dynamic — firms want to see 'difference' and customisation in management education to suit their needs.
	Market circumstances have redefined competition in management education. Recession and the reduction of public funds in combination with an over-supply of business school courses have prompted business schools to 'sharpen-up' their offerings to customers.
	Because university-based business schools have failed to deliver on management education, corporations are starting their own universities and incumbents shouldn't be surprised by this.

Table 7.6: Growth in the scale of management education provision.

Growth in management education	(Globalisation) The combination of transitioning economies and smaller businesses both demanding management skills has fuelled the growth of management education.
	The demand from fast-growing economies and the enterprises that follow this growth have supported growth in the market for management education.
	Globalisation coupled with social change in the west [has] led to more people going to university.
	There is a drive for professionalism in management and this has created demand for management qualifications from business schools.
	More companies and intensified competition meant that business schools were in demand to equip managers with skills and answer managerial problems. The broad socio-political forces of commoditisation and capitalism meant that business is central in most societies and this created demand for management education.

Table 7.7: The management education curriculum as a key issue.

Curriculum	Business ethics and CSR are on the public's mind far more than they used to be; there is a perceived 'ethics gap' in management education. This has acted as a demand-pull force on management education to incorporate these topics.
	When LBS and MBS were set up [in the United Kingdom], the original idea was that they would be very close to business, be very practical, not overly academic. Of course they couldn't be that because the whole ethos coming over from the US then was of the more academic, data-driven, research-based type of teaching, which is probably not totally suited to management teaching. The drive for academic legitimacy and to compete with US schools has formed a management curriculum that is not necessarily well-suited to teaching management.'
	A core problem with business school curricula is that they have a 'follower' attitude; they followed the trend into

Table 7.7: (*Continued*)

shareholder capitalism and now they're responding by trying to teach stakeholder capitalism. No business school stood up and said that shareholder approaches are wrong or dangerous until after the financial crisis.
In terms of developing management skills, business schools have been better at ensuring their own performance than they have at developing a purpose — there is still a lack of understanding of the relationship between business and society.

Table 7.8: The financial stability of the business school model as a key issue.

Financial stability of the business school model	We have an unjustifiable system based on research pushing schools up in the rankings — we all want to be in the best kind of business school — but this is a problem, one which needs to be paid for somehow.
	Only 1/3 of corporate sponsorship comes from companies, two-thirds comes from alumni. In the future it is anticipated that companies may provide less money. Thus there is an imperative to get companies involved with other activities — particularly research — and of business schools to move towards a more engaged relationship.

Table 7.9: Business school ranking as a key issue.

Ranking	There was a sense that the US had a (closed) set of rankings and that we (rest of world) didn't. It was business schools that said this is what we have to do (implement a ranking system).
	A proper and open and honest reflection on the global contribution of management education, e.g. examining what other schools do with a minimal resources, rather than sitting back and adopting a 'we're okay attitude' — that is, rankings show an obscured view of management education.

Globalisation is regarded as an important issue management education has to deal with. There are various (and distinct) facets to globalisation that make it a key issue:

- It has been the major factor in driving the demand for management education.
- A 'smaller world' has meant that the movement of students and faculty has become a key consideration for business schools.
- Established business schools (in a context of growing global demand for management education) have taken the opportunity to extend beyond their domestic territory.
- Globalisation has stimulated demand for 'international managers'.

There are concerns that a 'herd behaviour' exists in terms of some school's internationalisation with some going overseas to blindly follow the leaders and, hence, avoid being left behind but very often without a clear strategy for internationalisation.

Globalisation is many things to many people, but the key themes that relate to a global business environment are the high demand for management education, which means that business schools are challenged by the fluid movement of both students (customers) and of faculty (expertise). Consequently business schools are no longer anchored to their domestic base and customers increasingly demand international management skills for a globalised world environment.

The role of research and the interface between theory and practice in management education is perceived as another key issue. This can be subdivided into two strong themes. The first is that policy decisions about management education and its place within the university system have created an enduring need to prove its academic legitimacy through the production of rigorous research. The second is the concern that the kind of research conducted within management education is irrelevant to management practice.

The former compounds the latter as respondents identify the value (academic currency) attached to 'rigorous research', severely limiting management researchers' ability to produce research with relevance to practice. This rigour-relevance dilemma becomes even more problematic when, despite the intense pursuit of rigorous research, management is still seen as a minor intellectual player in relation to other academic (and professional) disciplines.

As well as the concern surrounding the practical relevance of management research for management practice, the pursuit of rigorous research is also seen as damaging the internal composition of business schools. The formation of disciplinary silos in business schools is seen as a result of organising for 'rigorous' research 'to move away from being vocationally oriented trade schools (Business 1.0) and to upgrade to play the university game'.

The established structures of Van Humbolt's discipline-based university make silos a necessary feature for business schools as part of the university system. However, the lack of fit and communication between management disciplines has led to a fragmented and over-specialised set of distinct sub-disciplines that are unable to 'talk' to one another in a way that benefits a multi-disciplinary view of management.

Respondents see the fact that business schools are in competition with one another as a key issue. Changes in the business environment of management education have increased competition; globalisation sees providers competing across borders in a globally competitive market. The competitive environment is also marked by a general decline in government funding. New entrants to the market are in the form of both corporate and for-profit universities.

Again, globalisation plays a role in influencing the nature of management education as it is seen as a key driver for the growth in the scale of management education throughout the world. Respondents point to a number of interrelated factors that have stimulated demand for management education. Broad social changes, such as a greater number of people going to university, have helped increase demand. The central importance given to business in many economies compounds the demand for skilled managers and, in turn, management education.

There is a feeling that management education does not meet the purpose of creating better managers. There are several underlying issues as to why this is the case.

- First, the pursuit of academic legitimacy has created conditions where business schools are engaged in the study *of* management rather than studies *for* better management. This is manifest in the concentration of resources on research (for publication in 'arcane' elite journals) as opposed to teaching and pedagogy.
- Second, business schools tend to react to management trends and broader external issues rather than shaping the management agenda (e.g. sustainable management practice).
- Third, business schools do not fully understand the role of business in society and are therefore ill equipped to teach better (responsible/sustainable) management practice.

> One of the problems is that research costs and if we expect 40% of our faculty time to be on research, or maybe even more, that has to be paid for and it is paid for out of very high

fees. ... Getting that balance between the requirement of research, teaching and practice right is a big challenge.

I have to say that, for us, the experience that we have here is that, of our fundraising efforts and campaigns, companies represent only about one-third of the corporate sponsorship that we have. So two-thirds actually comes from alumni; it's not a small thing but I don't think that we have to exaggerate the importance of companies in terms of fund raising. And I think that we are going to see the same thing in the future. Companies are not going to have more resources to give to universities — on the contrary, they may have fewer resources.

Some respondents cite business school ranking as a key issue in management education yet only a few go on to expand further on how rankings came to be an issue. This appears to indicate that rankings are a key issue but it is not clear what led to their emergence other than media interest in the field of management education and in the quality of outcomes achieved by it.

7.4. What Lessons Can be Learned from the Past?

With the main issues in management education and the drivers for their emergence identified, we asked respondents what lessons could be learned from the past.

It is particularly striking that the majority of respondents dwell more on negative than positive lessons. They identify negative aspects — *things that business schools have not achieved nor explicitly addressed* — as opposed to any positive impacts (of organisational learning) that management education may have had. From the positive responses, one individual identified that: 'I think that the industry overall has proven to be adaptive to change and to being a novelty. I think that's pretty clear'.

However, this runs contrary to other perceptions from the interview data. A second more widely articulated positive basis for learning can be found in the enduring value of the early phases of research and academic writing and insights on management:

I have a feeling that most of the things that were done in the past still have a value today. What we have to do is to continue to adapt them to the way business, society and technology are evolving. But in the end. ... I still think that the basic disciplines in management, the functional views, are still valued; I mean people need to know about these 'technicalities'.

Indeed, the research and written contributions that helped to define management as a field of study are still valuable today. However, the majority of responses suggest that there are significant gaps or shortfalls in what management education delivers — leading to much introspection and debate about future options for its evolution.

> I believe that you can learn quite a lot from the past by reflecting on issues that still seem to be there.

The responses are grouped into four categories corresponding to the answers given by interviewees (Figure 7.1). These themes are frequently interrelated (e.g. the structure of business schools provides a good fit with specialised, yet irrelevant, research but does not have a good fit with their perceived role within society).

The categories are as follows:

- Mission and purpose of business schools
- Knowledge production

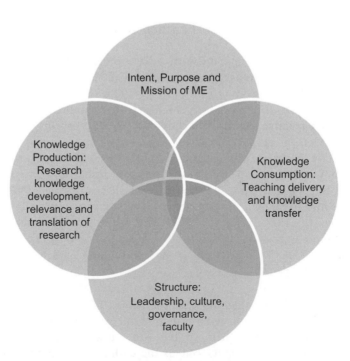

Figure 7.1: Areas where lessons can be learned in management education.

- Knowledge consumption (these encompasses the whole remit of research and teaching in all its various guises)
- Structural arrangements they operate within (e.g. the connection with universities, the prevalence of departmental silos as well as the competitive environment)

7.4.1.   Purpose/Mission

This area covers the overarching intent, mission and purpose of management education in the context of higher education, including the role and clear purpose of the business school, the relationship with business and the interface between business, government and society.

The quotations below reflect views stating that there needs to be a renewed sense of purpose involving radical rethinking of a revitalised educational philosophy embracing all stakeholders and being less inward looking and complacent:

> I think there needs to be a clearer sense of purpose and with that I focus on the wider human being.

> We need a stronger context for management education and a stronger sense of purpose why we're doing it.

> Management education has 'no meaning without context'.

> I think the lessons it can learn are that there needs to be another radical shift. ... We have to find new terrain.

> We tend not to study history in management education, which is quite interesting. ... I think it has probably been too much of a slave to a fairly one-dimensional view of philosophy.

> I think that we are doomed if we isolate ourselves, that we become stale by defining management education as the functions of operations, finance, marketing, whatever, with a bit of strategy to integrate it. We become so inward looking and complacent like with any other business [that] needs to change ... to be challenged by society.

> Over the last 20 years there's been a focus on shareholder value and I remember being quite shocked when in one American school, students seemed quite delighted that in

response to one case study the solution was to fire the workforce. It seems like a wrong mindset — it's cruel. That kind of teaching has to be stopped. We have to take a more humane approach to how we manage a company, what we think management is and the purpose of the corporation. There are other people involved not just the shareholders.

7.4.2. Knowledge Production

This area focuses on knowledge development and the role of management research in enriching management education. One of the abiding concerns is the gap between rigorous management research and the practice of management (research and knowledge development, research relevance and translation to stakeholders, consultancy and management problem solving):

> One of the things that I fear about our discipline-based approach is that we are reinventing the wheel in covering the disciplines but don't actually know very much about history … [whereas] actually in the disciplines the problems have remained fundamentally the same. Scholars had fine-tuned their perspectives on it in a number of different ways but there wasn't a lot new. And so I fear that in a lot of cases what we do is train these young people up and then they start reinventing problems and they think that they are the first to address these issues. And if they had done more than a cursory search, they'd realise that, pretty much invariably, all of this stuff is talked about fully, wisely and profoundly by others who preceded them. So I fear that we don't have a good institutional memory.

> [A business school] should never assume that it is the only place where management research takes place.

> You cannot run a business school so disconnected from the business world in terms of programmes, research and staying in touch with the real world. And a healthy school is part of a dynamic network of companies, recruiters, graduate students and entrepreneurs. You have to be there and contribute to this network, and somehow benefit as well from it, mainly through ideas.

This is the knowledge learning approach between managers and educators. [There is a] need for a balanced approach; [it's] too abstract at present.

The research we do should be to some degree engage with the world of management practice ... otherwise you are not a business and management school.

7.4.3. Knowledge Consumption

This is the area where the content of management education is examined and where teaching and the high-quality transfer of knowledge drawn from research takes place (e.g. teaching and knowledge transfer, impact on practice/policy, and relevance to business and management).

There is considerable reflection in the respondent's comments about the proper delivery of management education. There are real concerns about the content, the narrowness of current instructional approaches and the use of methods such as case studies, which focus on past practices and ignore future concerns and instructional relevance.

Case teaching harks back to the past, established practices and identifies them but does not identify how to focus on the future. ... I like to focus on not necessarily taking established wisdom but to try to engage minds to think more freely and not accept [but] challenge.

I think it's about giving people, young people, the ability to apply what they have learned and to give them the ability to learn, not so much in the sense of 'I know my financial models' ... but enhancing the ability to understand and learn.

We've narrowed down instruction in business education to convergent thinking and have neglected the breadth. ... In only a few cases do management problems yield to convergent thinking. ... I think the interplay between convergent and divergent thinking is important.

I think that someone else said this: "We shouldn't just teach the tools we should teach how to use the tools"; to teach responsibly, ethically and for the general good of mankind really, rather than being too narrow.

Learning should not be teaching in silos/subject areas. We may need to start teaching in silos but we have to be more integrative and paint a much more holistic picture. We need to achieve far more synthesis across the subject areas. We must focus more on the development of individuals rather than bits of theory.

It should recognise that its research is increasingly considered irrelevant by those it seeks to understand and by that I mean policy makers, senior managers and influential people in business who are going to shape the future of this world.

The main lesson has to do with the fact that management has to be relevant, and that means in terms of relevance and training. History is very important in terms of understanding cycles such as why are the banks making the same mistakes as 10 years ago? I think that these are very important issues and there needs to be an ability to learn from and appreciate experiments instead of saying this is right or wrong. Failure is even more helpful than success. It's all a matter of learning from experiments. It's never either a total failure or a total success.

Don't offer off-the-shelf products. Understand your market better. Truly customise your programmes for clients' needs.

I think that action learning has a great part to play in our education and we don't use it nearly enough because it is difficult to deliver and difficult to assess. But I really do think that it's a lot about vocational training, skills that can really only be learned by doing in my opinion. You can't learn it out of a textbook. But I do think that we've moved from the very informal education to one which is much more formal.

7.4.4. Structure

This area is concerned with the aspects of strategic change in management education. How do existing organisational structures, faculty cultures and governance systems address willingness to change? What is the role of leadership in improving the quality and performance of a business school? These include organisational structure (leadership, culture, governance), relationship with universities, faculty employment model, business model and competition.

Business schools themselves can be barriers to change. They can kill creativity and innovation and operate in narrow silos (departments) that discourage integration and multi-discipline co-operation.

> Institutions kill creativity — do we have people today who are larger than life in business education? Are we rewarding administrators and bureaucrats? Do we in the academy discourage those who create friction (new ideas) — that friction is essential.

> The 'one model fits all approach' has gone.

> History teaches you something about how organisations are run. One of the things that I've always thought is odd is the lack of reflexivity in management schools. They don't apply what they teach about other organisations to themselves. You don't have the strategy professors having a really good influence on the strategy of the business school. You don't have the marketing professors having good input on the marketing of the school. It could be because they are not thinking about how their organisation functions. I raise this to answer your question in terms of how organisations have functioned in the past can help you to understand how the organisation is functioning now.

Within the sector, there is a sense from respondents that competition — or lack of co-operation — between schools has undermined the potential of management education:

> Management education has historically not been global and the way that we operated in the past isn't the way we'll operate in the future because it doesn't emphasise collaboration, developing this global-ready graduate. So what we've had in the past is isolation and a lack of co-operation. We've got to move forward towards integration so we can draw on that from the past.

> I like competing as a team towards a certain goal. I don't like the model where killing the other is the objective. In EFMD we have this kind of approach to partners with other organisations rather than fighting against each other. ... There is no single organisation that can do everything. For example, I would rather see a school that is focusing on one aspect and

becomes very good at that rather than trying to have a whole range of programmes.

Lack of change is also a key aspect of respondent comments across three areas, namely knowledge production, mission/purpose and faculty. Resistance to change in knowledge production could be seen as a consequence of methodological conservatism, increasing rigour and 'unusable' research despite the success of business schools in the 1980s. There is a sense that little has changed in the context of management education (old case studies, little innovation/idea generation) and the dominance of faculty governance and resistance to change remains:

> I think that case studies — will case studies still be here? We seem to do it the same as we did 100 years ago — not just 20 years ago. It is still the same stuff. And we should be out there in front of companies not following them. If you talk about the physics department or medicine, they are actually creating stuff the whole time, they're not analysing what's happened.

> I think that they can learn by looking back not too far, perhaps to the 1970s and 1980s when business schools were seen as the future. This was where academic relevance and rigour came together, this was where businesses and organisations of all kinds were able to discuss and develop ideas with academics and I think that it's time to, if not to revisit that, then have a similar kind of shift.

> The biggest problem has got to be willingness to accept change — and it's hard to induce a culture of constant change among faculty and students. Everybody tends to be cautious — 'caution' is often the major watchword. We like to think of ourselves as risk-takers but as a group of people we tend to be the smallest risk-takers in the world.

> Faculty find it difficult to think beyond the context; they think of what is being done now, they can't see that down the road management education might be about something different. Academics have the most conservative approach to anything.

> I think that you have a lot of faculty members making a lot of money with outside activities. How do you actually make

faculty members feel that their first duty is towards the school? But also how do you engage them in useful and challenging projects so that those people spend more time at the school, especially senior faculty members? I do think that's something we have to deal with.

7.5. What Lessons Have Not Been Learned?

Respondents' answers can be considered in the context of the four elements that surfaced in our discussion of the key issues of management education: mission/purpose of management education, knowledge production, knowledge consumption and structural aspects of the sector.

The responses about the lessons not learned, or gaps, in management education covered the following points:

- Lack of a clear identity, philosophy and purpose in management education
- Processes of knowledge production in which management research lacks relevance, impact and influence
- Processes of knowledge consumption, which need changes in management curricula focusing particularly on liberal values (ethics, CSR, moral philosophy) and embracing management needs in areas of technology enhancement and innovation
- Structural changes to limit the growth of silos and faculty-led governance and to create new business models led by strong and courageous leaders

7.5.1. Mission/Purpose of Management Education

There is a clear view that business schools are complacent. The mission of the business school is seen as generally too narrow and focused. It does not espouse a distinct philosophy and is not anchored well in terms of broad societal influence. It lacks a coherent agenda and the lessons of history have not been learned:

> I simply believe that we have not yet learned how to react to the big problems in society.

> Through history you get insights into human beings and social developments, which also are really relevant in mastering today's reality or that for the future.

> I remember going to one of my earliest EQUIS reviews where there was a Frenchman on the team who said: 'Where's the

philosophy in this degree?' ... I think that it is not necessarily about philosophy but about a much broader brush that locates management in management education within the gambit of what human beings do.

Business schools have the theoretical ability to be proactive and shape agendas, either by themselves or in consortia or through their societies. But really haven't seized that at all. They've become, in my view, pretty complacent across Europe and that's not helped by the fact that the top business schools in Europe have remained in the same small grouping for the last 30 or 40 years.

7.5.2. *Knowledge Production and Relevance*

Business schools have not yet learned to produce research that addresses the needs and problems of management practice. The obsessive physics-envy (scientific rigour) approach is unfit for purpose in management education and there needs to be a balance between rigour and managerial relevance:

> We are in a mode where the quantity, quality and emphasis on research are slowly declining. Some people may say that's good or bad — not wasting time on esoteric things [though] on a peer comparison with universities it is going to put us at a disadvantage. Business schools should be a place where research does take place. We have slowly de-emphasised that.

> We generally thought that you could optimise everything; I don't think that you can. Things like emotional capital and so on are important because you can inspire people. A lot of what we are teaching is training people to be boring. A lot of management education is boring.

> Business schools or institutions of management development have not learned to keep pace with companies; I think they're behind them. And they use as their excuse [not] relevance but rigour. But I think this is just an excuse to slow it down. I have nothing against academic research but when you are dealing with a client that moves at the speed of light sometimes and you have the academic world that moves much slower, they haven't learned that there's nothing wrong sometimes with doing a report a bit more quickly.

What hasn't been learned is that rarefied, irrelevant research just can't be at the heart of the system. That's the big one!

7.5.3. *Knowledge Production, Technology and Innovation*

As already noted, the kind of management taught in business schools does not reflect the practice of management in the 'real world', particularly in the areas of innovation and technology. This is reflected in the views of business stakeholders who, as employers, say that students are not prepared for managerial careers. As (potential) knowledge consumers, they say that the research produced is irrelevant and does not solve the business problems they currently face. Technology and the whole area of management innovation are under-researched areas where theory and teaching no longer reflect contemporary management practice:

> I don't think we've been very good about linking management to technology, about communications technology; we tend to treat management as a bit isolated and yet what's happening out there is they're making use of all these technologies in a way that we don't really take into account in business schools.

> I would say that management education is ripe for innovation (and destructive technology). You can't just sit there. ... The top schools are hampered by heritage. ... I think all the innovation is going to come from the second-tier and third-tier schools.

7.5.4. *Knowledge Consumption: At What Stage of Management Development Is Management Education Appropriate for Students?*

We may only now be recognising the need for the design of management education as a lifelong process. Respondents raise the issue of what form of management education may be appropriate during an individual's lifetime. The challenge (or appropriateness) of management education for masses of undergraduate students and an increasingly young MBA cohort has prompted some respondents to consider whether it belongs at 'the beginning' — early in being, or before becoming, a manager. Post-experience courses and models for lifelong learning may add considerable value to the impact of management education. The MBA, for example, could be regarded as an entry point and not a driving licence for a management career:

I think that we have learned something but we can do much better. Something we have to do is to learn what kind of integration is needed at what stage in the career of a person. You need a different kind of integration when you deal with a 40 year old than when you deal with a 23 year old.

[For business you need] a certain level of education, which you absolutely need in order to be a manager who can survive in modern society. And for that the MBA is a very useful thing. But to me it has become the beginning and not the end.

7.5.5. Knowledge Consumption: What Exactly Is the Content of Management Education and What Is It For?

Business schools struggle with whether management is a discipline. They have not learned how to teach and instil values in managers that meet the expectations of stakeholders — there is increasing pressure on schools to improve management behaviour and to play their part in improving and reforming the relationships businesses have with their stakeholders and society. This is especially true where the figures at the centre of scandals often hold MBAs from prestigious schools:

Management as an academic discipline doesn't really exist. It is an amalgamation of a number of disciplines.

We seem to downgrade the importance of practice-based education and action-based learning. Perhaps one way of doing this would be a potential innovation in which we set up the curriculum that would involve, or require, the faculty to go along on an action-based journey with their study.

[Something] I have learned over the last 20 years is the constant challenge by society of the ethical behaviour of our students and frankly speaking we have no good answer to that. We have the easy answer that ethics is something you learn before you come to business school; you learn it as a child. It is a poor answer. It's a cop out.

I think that we constantly crash into the fact that rational management and profit maximisation can often end in tears. You need a visible hand not an invisible hand. We seem constantly surprised that another recession has come around or that some other schmuck has created a mega-scandal.

I don't think that we're as realistic as we need to be about the base human drivers. You can't trust all of the people all of the time.

I do think that we've lost sight of the teaching of skills and I keep coming back to this because I think that the role and purpose of business schools is to develop the next generation of business leaders. They need to be equipped with knowledge, certainly, but they also need to be equipped with the "how to" experience. And we haven't kept pace with that. We've become too research focused.

We haven't learned how to educate our managers whether they're young managers or mid-career learners in taking a wider perspective. But maybe that's a challenge of capitalism rather than of business education.

7.5.6. Knowledge Consumption: Impact

The debates about the rigour and relevance of management education and research are well rehearsed and covered by respondents throughout our sample. We tend to focus on relatively narrow intellectual contributions or (minor) changes to management practice as indicators of impact. However, the broader impact that business schools have on public or private organisations is considered to be very marginal.

I don't think that business schools realise or recognise that actually they're relatively marginal players in terms of the things they feel they do influence. They don't influence large organisations, commercial organisations or public sector organisations any more. They don't have a strong voice in public or private policy [or] in the development of world economics and globalisation, no matter how much they use those words. They are not the slightest influence [on] policy makers and government.

7.5.7. Structure and Knowledge Consumption: The Effects of Silos

One respondent argues that the effect of teaching in disciplinary silos leads to a false, narrow impression of management. Even if business schools teach

each subject discipline to an excellent standard, not enough is done to join the dots and integrate understanding about the nature of management in business and society. If business schools are too focused on the hard, rational skills demanded by each discipline, then broader ethical and societal implications of management behaviour are missed and are potential blind spots for management education:

> If you teach finance, for example, you also need to teach the linkages that it isn't finance for finance's sake. Students need to understand what this actually means out in the real world: it isn't just equations and investing in stocks and shares, or doing NPV calculations. If you're talking about a general management degree, then I think that you do have to start with the silos but I think that one course at the end on Business Policy is not sufficient to cross the silos.

7.5.8.   *Structural: The Power of Faculty*

There is a clear view that faculty within schools are too powerful and are resistant to the kinds of changes that would begin to address the issues at the heart of the business school debate, for example:

> I think that we know that some of the things that go on in business schools are mainly for the benefit of the producers, the faculty, and we know that and we don't seem to do anything about it, so that's a lesson that has not been learned. The business model doesn't appear to be working that well and yet nobody has said how we are going to fix it. [But] let's try to fix it; people seem to take the approach that it will all work out in the end.

And, with respect to faculty governance, one respondent noted that changes in the business model and necessary strategic changes require strong, courageous leadership of business schools:

> There is a lack of courage. We are in a world where good schools need good leaders, with the same competence we require from leaders of business.

Chapter 8

Change in Management Education: What Are the Barriers to Change in Management Education and Triggers for Change in the Future?

8.1. Introduction

In a changing social and political environment one of the clear lessons of the past is the need to adjust the 'business model' of the business school in relation to mission, purpose, governance, and knowledge development and transfer. We, therefore, asked respondents to identify the barriers to change in management education.

Table 8.1 ranks the responses while Table 8.2 clusters them into a number of thematic groups that are examined in greater detail.

8.2. What Issues Are Seen as 'Barriers to Change'?

A brief summary of the findings on the 'barriers to change' provokes the following observations:

- First, the dominant barriers to change (62%) for management education (at least for university-based business schools) arise from the nature of the university system and its related features. The university system itself, the relative power and resistance to change by faculty, and the pressures of academic rigour feature as dominant barriers to change.
- Second, issues related to leadership account for over one-fifth (22%) of the barriers identified by respondents. The major area for concern was the level of risk aversion and conservatism seen throughout management education.

Table 8.1: Barriers to change in management education.

Barriers	Number	Percentage
Faculty	11	34
University system	10	31
Risk aversion	8	25
Academic rigour	6	19
Promotion and tenure	3	9
Disciplinary silos	3	9
Lack of resources	3	9
Accreditation	2	6
Leadership	2	6
Rankings	1	3
Valuing teaching	1	3
Research assessment	1	3
Government	1	3
Complacency	1	3
Short termism	1	3
Ourselves — business schools	1	3

Number of respondents = 32.

Table 8.2: Barriers to change in thematic groups.

Barriers	Related issues	Number	Cumulative total	Cumulative percentage of responses
University system		10	10	
	Faculty	11	21	
	Promotion and tenure	3	24	
	Academic rigour	6	30	
	Disciplinary silos	3	33	
	Valuing teaching	1	34	
				62
Leadership		2	2	
	Risk aversion	8	10	
	Complacency	1	11	
	Short termism	1	12	
				22

Table 8.2: (*Continued*)

Barriers	Related issues	Number	Cumulative total	Cumulative percentage of responses
Rankings		1	1	
	Accreditation	2	3	
	Research assessment	1	4	
				7
Government		1	1	
	Lack of resources	3	4	
				7
Others		0	0	
	Ourselves-business schools	1	1	
				2

Note: Thirty-two responses yielded 55 barriers to change.

- Third, issues concerned with the performance of schools in rankings, research assessment and accreditation accounted for 7% of the barriers.
- Fourth, government and the widespread reduction of state funding and resources for business schools accounted for a further 7%.
- Finally, a few respondents saw business schools in their current format, that is the current 'business model' itself, to be a barrier to change. This can be considered a combination of the other four issues; the structure, leadership, performance indicators and lack of resources were seen to make business schools resistant to change. Elements of this resistance include inertia, complacency, conservatism, the academic mind set (e.g. elitism, university politics, the need for consensus, mistrust of bureaucracy) and risk aversion.

8.2.1. The University System

Fragueiro and Thomas (2011, pp. 56–57) note that Mintzberg's (2007) work on strategic decision processes classifies the business school as a professional form of organisation akin to a professional service firm. Bryman (2007) also notes that academics in higher education react against a directive style of overt leadership since it would interfere with their own authority. Mintzberg confirms that academics prefer a covert form of leadership that preserves their autonomy and creates an environment of critical debate, collegiality and consensus-based decisions. However, this form of leadership may create impedance to change and an inherent conservatism. Some of this is evident in the following comments:

> The influence of the university in university-based business schools is too strong. [It] is too financially burdensome for the school. If a school can't keep its own money to invest, that can make it very difficult to change anything.

> [There are the] limitations of the broader academic structures outside the business school in a university. Integrated business schools can draw on knowledge — the intellectual rigour of universities — but [are] emasculated by petty resource and political issues between business schools, other disciplines and other university departments. [But] autonomous business schools continually lack academic and intellectual rigour because they are not part of an intellectual university environment.

> [There is a] general inertia, which I think has to do with universities and their view of business schools, and the fact that business schools have had it relatively easy for some time as long as they make enough money. And I think that that is a bad contract because it does two things: creates complacency among the business schools; and creates a very strange bond of trust or mistrust between the university and other departments. And I think that that is very, very, unhealthy.

> … university professors look like they did 50 years ago — too autonomous. Independent thinkers belong to the academic family, not business.

8.2.2.   Faculty

As noted already, central to the leadership and organisation of academics is the 'management of autonomy' — faculty are seen as an important barrier to change:

> The entrenched positions of our faculty. That's it.

> I think that the barriers to change are probably ourselves, that is the people who work in business education. Mainly, probably, the faculty. I think that it is basically the faculty that is reluctant to see certain changes.

> [It's] the faculty because if you have this huge emphasis on research in the world in which we operate then inevitably it narrows people's focus. They have to publish to get promoted, therefore most often it is not productive to go too far beyond that and to think about linking across to philosophy, etc. Well ... some of them may be good at making linkages and doing interdisciplinary work but the vast majority are not. So that's the barrier.

> Faculty — they have to get behind it. We have switched to a more heterogeneous group of people and it's hard to get consensus.

Most discussions about faculty concern their relative power within management education, coupled with, in general, their resistance to change. Another barrier that surfaced was the quality and availability of PhDs — the worldwide shortage of well-trained doctoral-qualified faculty — to sustain the management education system.

8.2.3. Promotion and Tenure

Another element of the faculty structure in most business schools is the promotion and tenure system.

Promotion and tenure as part of university structures was identified as a clear barrier to change in management education. The system appears to exacerbate the tensions felt by business schools in providing rigorous research, yet needing also to offer high-quality, relevant teaching. It provides a misalignment between desired outcomes and rewards/incentives for faculty:

> [We lack] the ability to pick up from relevant research what should then be shaping our teaching. Why do we have those barriers? I think that a lot of it has to do with things like the promotion and tenure process, which is obsolete.

> [The problem with universities is], I think, the promotion and tenure process.

8.2.4. Leadership

The greatest leadership concern by respondents was the high level of risk aversion (and as noted earlier an absence of courage in leadership), which are seen to be driven by leaders both being part of the university system and the 'entrenched' position of faculty:

> I think that business schools are going to have to profes-
> sionalise when it comes to the management of their institutions
> [...] it's got to be somebody who can understand how a
> business school operates, who the faculty trust — in any
> change operation trust is extremely important — and you've
> also got to have a person who's interested in doing the job. If
> they don't have any curiosity or patience and will to get things
> done, it won't happen. So it's the faculty, but I also think that it
> is the way the management is put into place at the top of the
> business schools.

This creates two general consequences. First, deans (leaders) are often unwilling to upset the basis of their existing revenue streams. Second, the rift between management education and management practice is exacerbated as faculty stress rigorous, academic research rather than more relevant, practically oriented research; management education, and deans, are trailing behind in influencing management practice rather than taking an active and positive stance in shaping it:

> [Leaders] tend to be conservative in terms of revenue streams
> and what is generating them and we like to think that it is
> going to go on forever. [We] don't want to do anything that is
> likely to dissipate the ability to generate revenue. [They] have
> created Advisory Boards but sometimes these tend to impede
> our ability to be innovative in that anything we want to do has
> to be acceptable to them. I don't think that we can respond
> as quickly to things as we have to run it by everybody. One
> effect of empowering this stakeholder group has long-term
> implications in terms of our ability to make decisions and
> respond.
>
> I think that there is the financial reality. A school, a dean or a
> faulty member can have the perfect view of what ought to be
> done for society but in the meantime there are seats to be filled.
> It is a reality, unless of course there is extensive funding, that
> the institution has to attract students one way or the other.

Consequently, without courageous and path-breaking leaders, faculty will emphasise disciplinary over multi-disciplinary practical research:

> The leaders are the ones with most of the control. The faculty
> are brought up to be increasingly narrow and increasingly

more developed experts in a narrow part of a particular discipline. How then do we develop these 'globally aware' managers in our programmes if our faculty are narrow and anchored in their disciplines?

It is clear that among the lessons *not* learned from the past is that schools are perceived as followers rather than leaders in enhancing and generating management knowledge.

8.2.5. *Accreditation*

While accreditation processes can achieve improved business school quality, respondents indicate that they can also be a barrier to change through 'bureaucratic oversight' and pressures to make business schools the same; accreditation standards can lead to homogenous business models and membership of the 'status quo':

> It's bureaucratic oversight that is a huge barrier and certainly not creative. Because if you don't fit in a slot you run the risk of having your programme, or your degree or your school lose its accreditation ... I think, certainly, some other accrediting agencies have got huge barriers. The whole box-checking exercise is one that might give people comfort that all the boxes are checked but does it really advance the cause?

> The fact that we have these international rating bodies is making a kind of isomorphism for the industry, which means there is a more dominant mode or way of structuring a business school. I think that we need to allow for more variation depending on the missions and the context of business schools. So a barrier can be the lack of well-established models for the different kinds of business school missions ... If you are in an emerging market and your mission is to strongly contribute to economic development in your region or country, probably you will manage faculty and research in a quite different way than the accrediting bodies will establish.

8.2.6. *Lack of Resources*

With the worldwide decline in public funding, private and corporate funding sources become very important for business schools. A lack of resources, or the lack of ability to compete for resources, is seen by one respondent as a direct product of the lack of relevance in management research:

> Lack of success in research in business and management has not attracted research grants and is not seen by business as relevant to the practice of management.

And, for another respondent, it is a secondary concern after management education's inbuilt resistance to change:

> I'd like to say that higher education just doesn't get enough money to do the things it needs to do but that's really the second point I'd make … The first point is that the industry is built to be resistant to change.

8.3.   What Is Likely to Trigger Change in the Future?

Having identified both the barriers to change and the resistance to change in business schools we were curious to identify what might trigger change in the future.

Our respondents see the triggers for change in management education arising from three areas shown in Table 8.3 but predominately from Funding and Sustainability of the Business Model.

- First, funding issues and the sustainability of the business model in management education noted by 42% of respondents.
- Second, competition within the industry mentioned by 23% of respondents.
- Third, faculty-related triggers stated by 23% of respondents.

Below, we provide some more detailed insight into the six most frequent triggers for change: funding and sustainability, competition, faculty, exogenous shocks, and technology and leadership, using quotations from selected respondents.

Table 8.3: Triggers of change in management education.

Trigger	Number	Percentage
Funding and the sustainability of the business model for management education	11	42
Competition	6	23

Table 8.3: (*Continued*)

Trigger	Number	Percentage
Faculty related	6	23
• Shortage of faculty (3)		
• Training of faculty (1)		
• Faculty incentives (1)		
• Cost of faculty (1)		
Exogenous shock	5	19
Technology	4	15
Political factors	3	12
Leadership	3	12
Student choice	2	8
Research assessment	1	4
Financial sustainability	1	4
Accreditation	1	4
Growth of management Education	1	4
Ranking	1	4
Innovation in ME	1	4
Interdisciplinary ways of working	1	4

8.3.1.   *Funding and Sustainability*

The first trigger of change is associated with the continuing funding problems in higher education. Just under half of respondents suggest that a key trigger of change is connected with the availability of resources, specifically funding expensive faculty in business schools in a climate of increasing global competition and declining government funding for higher education. This, they believe, will prompt change within management education and stimulate the search for a new set of business models that will establish new and more viable competitive positions:

> Some business schools are going to go bust at some point, and some may have come close to it already. [There are] 12,000 business schools in the world — I can't believe they're all going to stay profitable. That will trigger change.

> I think that you'll see schools disappearing. Pity the poor school in the UK that can't charge £9,000. I don't know how they are going to survive. The public universities, of course, are going to suffer first because they're not going to be getting the

money from the governments and they've been so used to the public trough that they don't know how to operate without it.

Without having enough money, either you get innovative, which certainly means broader use of technology, or you run a cost structure that is not sustainable, certainly tuition is sure to go up but there's a resistance to that too.

Judy Olian at UCLA said we're a borderline school here, we're not Harvard, but we're a very good school. You can perhaps put Warwick and Manchester in the same category in the UK, which is that of very good schools doing a very good job. But they're the ones who will survive — there's the rubbish cheap ones at the other end. But to keep paying faculty for doing all the things that you need to do to maintain educational standards, the books don't balance, do they?

Some business schools are just not going to make it financially. They are not going to recruit enough students, they are not going to be able to balance the books, they are going to come under increasing scrutiny to see if they can do that by their mother university. And I think that will be a trigger; but it will not be the only trigger.

The person who comes up with a better business model that actually works is going to be the trigger for change. The big trigger is going to be the person who gets across this barrier and figures out how he or she is going to do more of these things, get scale economies at a lower cost, because cost is going to be the one big long-term problem we're going to have because costs are going to way outstrip our generated revenues.

8.3.2. Competition Within the Industry

There is a shared belief that competition will increase in the industry and that heightened competition will force some changes within management education. Competition appears to have a broad set of bases: removing complacency from the industry and identifying new business models, is one pressure facing incumbents; privatisation and global competition for students and resources are cited as key triggers of change:

The punters [are] walking away from it. People will need to be more competitive.

> Competition forces rethinking of options, shakes the tree, removes complacency.

> I think that market pressure is going to become much more important. So I think that business schools are going to be compelled to change, partly because of privatisation and globalisation and the corresponding market pressures. I think that there is going to be one critical driver and it's the pressure to change.

> I think that we will see some business schools actually moving forward, doing new things. I don't know whether those things are going to be successful but what INSEAD has been doing in Asia, this is something that is changing the way some of us actually think.

However, if the position of business schools continues to be considered irrelevant (or too specialised) there is some concern that competition will not exist between business schools but between other players in the market such as management consultants and business analysts.

> We mustn't forget management consultants and business analysts. One thing that has happened in the last 20 years or so that I've noticed, and strikingly, is that business analysts become consultants and come to the fore in a way that I certainly hadn't appreciated was around in the 1970s for example. And there's an almost vicious circle going on where business schools do the research, consultancies take the researchers out to dinner, the research is then condensed into a two-by-two matrix or a similar easy package and then sold on. And that's not a criticism; that's simply their business. But I think that the impact of business analysts, economic analysts and management consultants is also a massive threat to what business schools currently do. Because if I were a CEO, I would probably go to PWC or McKinsey rather than INSEAD.

8.3.3. Faculty-Related Triggers

Faculty and the promotion and tenure system are viewed as additional triggers of change. This encompasses the cost of faculty, the demographic crisis and the reduction in the supply of PhD graduates from major schools, creating a shortage of faculty. Further, there is the problem of how to align incentives and reward systems for faculty with changes to management education:

> The sheer difficulty of attracting faculty at a reasonable cost will make big changes. There'll be far more associate lecturers and people brought in.

> A dearth of faculty talent — a lot more faculty are needed across the world. I think that there'll be a crisis.

This relates to the triggers seen in the funding and sustainability of the business model in management education. In terms of an impending shortage of high-quality faculty, respondents saw this as a likely trigger of change:

> Resources are not only financial. The scarcity of faculty is going to be something that is also going to cause this. You are not going to have enough faculty, from what I understand, to fill all the positions in the schools, so it's difficult ... no one's figured out a way yet to run a business school without faculty.

> I think that there are schools that ought not to be around. And yes, I think that it is a good thing. There ought to be much more quality around our business schools rather than just being physical resources that attract students and student money. I also think that we could have such an acute shortage of faculty that we'd be far better having less students and schools that are fully staffed with quality academics rather than having to make do and mend and bring in sessional people.

However, one respondent saw a very positive element in the faculty situation. New faculty bring in a momentum for change in the faculty balance:

> New faculty coming on board, new ideas ... that's what brings changes.

And another European respondent argues that great academics can influence curricula and research significantly:

> Great ideas, new ideas ... so when Professor Kenneth Andrews (Harvard Business School) came out with the idea of strategy ... strategic thinking changed management education in my view.

8.3.4. *Exogenous Shocks*

Close to 20% of respondents thought that the trigger for change in management education would have to come from outside of management education and provide a 'shock' to the current system. The notion that a shock is needed corresponds to the belief that business schools are slow to change and have a large component of organisational inertia, which means it will take a significant external shock to prompt change:

> I'm almost convinced that something external is going to have to cause it because there's almost too much weight, too much momentum right now to continue doing what we're always doing.

> External events will shape a lot of it and make people go back to basics and think about what we are trying to do. They've been carried away on a wave of apparent success that is not evaluated.

> There's an interesting argument by a Canadian economist, Jeff Rubin, who suggests that if oil prices get too high, we will stop moving products around the world. Too high could be $200–$250 per barrel. At some point it is more economically sensible to produce at home than to produce abroad and ship stuff, especially the double shipping of things, the raw materials come from one country to another for production and then shipped back. The point may come when it is no longer feasible to do this ... So I think that as the oil and energy prices continue to become astronomical, this will have a huge effect on the way business is done and on the way business schools operate in terms of both educational content but also how are we shipping our people back and forth, bringing people to us.

Some respondents perceive the need for a sharp external change in order to instigate change in management education. This may involve a crisis such as the financial meltdown or a scandal such as ENRON, resulting in an increasing focus on ethics and moral/social responsibility in management education curricula. Alternatively, external corporate strategies focused on mergers/acquisitions may emerge:

> Oh, I think it will come from the outside. I think you are going to have things like mergers (e.g. SKEMA in France, AALTO in Finland) with business schools coming together. I think you will also see acquisitions.

8.3.5. Technology and Innovation

There is a clear view among respondents that technology and innovation have real potential to trigger changes in teaching delivery, research opportunities and network organisations in business schools. Yet much of this technological change needs to be more fully exploited — students are seen as more technology savvy than their professors:

> I think that the next generation of innovation will no more be a combination of existing technologies ... it will create an innovation — we will have to go back to our roots.

> I think that the potential re-definition of the role of professor, which can be caused by effective learning technologies and methodologies, again may challenge things. This always happens.

> Changing into having more interdisciplinary work with technology and engineering. As the world becomes more technological, then management has to be able to handle that rather better than they have so far. I think that will happen.

> I think that students feel that business schools are technologically out of the ark.

> I think widely distributed knowledge through the internet will change the way we think and work and do things and this will push through into management education. The notion of research publishing will change utterly over the next 10–20 years.

8.3.6. Leadership

And, finally, some respondents see leadership as a critical element in strategic reorientation and change. Leaders need to have courage and take risks:

> Leadership — to do strategic change we need leaders to be aware of changes that are needed or ongoing and influence academics.

> Leaders who are risk takers will trigger change.

Very few business school deans have the courage to say what's actually going on ... they're sitting there and hoping that it will come back.

8.4. Can We Change Management Education?

Given the sometimes-conflicting viewpoints of stakeholders and the many issues and lessons not learned that they identify, it is appropriate to ask whether change in management education is possible at all. Will the barriers *to* change dominate the triggers and pressures *for* change?

Our evidence indicates a common concern about revitalising curricula and encouraging diversity in teaching and learning approaches. In addition, there is a felt need to understand, through the lessons of history, how business schools got it wrong during the global financial crisis and to stimulate rankings/accreditation agencies to focus more deeply on schools' educational distinctiveness and programmes rather than a value proposition stressing growth in graduate salaries and reputation.

However, it is evident that business schools occupy a difficult position in attempting to straddle the conflicting goals of academic legitimacy and identity and management practice where arguably the needs of neither are met! Crainer and Dearlove caricature this predicament, portraying business schools as schizophrenic organisations that must demonstrate their capacity as 'bona fide' academic institutions, improve knowledge to provide practical solutions to management problems and at the same time perform as businesses.

But, the key question is whether business schools will exhibit a willingness to change and adopt a new approach to management education. One problem central to answering this question is the quality of leadership by deans and other academic leaders with respect to faculty and staff in business schools.

The problem is about the potential deficit of strategic leadership in many business schools. Deans have been variously described as 'jugglers', 'dictators', 'doves of peace' and 'dragons'. Their roles are seen as multi-faceted, stressful and often characterised as similar to middle managers squeezed between university presidents and demanding faculty members. Further, deans face short tenures (the median tenure of a business school dean is only three to four years), ambitious goals and critical challenges as they lead schools towards their future evolution.

As a consequence particularly of time pressure, many deans will probably 'muddle through' and make incremental minor changes to their existing business schools models. A few who have experience, time and the courage, determination and resilience to follow through their chosen path and strategic direction succeed. Success is personified by leaders such as Bain, Borges and Lorange (Fragueiro & Thomas, 2011). They reach the quality level described by Jim Collins as Level 5 leaders who possess 'a paradoxical combination of personal humility and professional will'. These are the great leaders who leave behind lasting legacies.

References

Agnelli, G. (1996). P. 117 in EFMD. (1996). *Training the fire brigade: Preparing for the unimaginable.* Brussels, Belgium: EFMD Publications.

Antunes, D., & Thomas, H. (2007). The competitive disadvantages of European business schools. *Long Range Planning, 40*(3), 392–404.

Bain, G. (1996). P. 89 in EFMD (1996) (op. cit.).

Bryman, A. (2007). Effective leadership in higher edcation: a literature reveiw. *Studies in Higher Education, 32*(6), 693–710.

Canals, J. (Ed.). (2011). *The future of leadership development.* Basingstoke UK: Palgrave Macmillan. (See Chapter 1.1, pp. 3–31).

Crainer, S., & Dearlove, D. (1998). *Gravy training.* Oxford, UK: Capstone Publishing.

Danos, P. (2011). Foreword. In S. Iniguez (Ed.), *The learning curve.* London: Palgrave Macmillan.

EFMD. (1976). *Pocock report on education and training needs of Europe's managers.* Brussels, Belgium: EFMD Publications.

EFMD. (1977). *Honko report on supply and demand of faculty.* Brussels, Belgium: EFMD Publications.

EFMD. (1978). *Moucret report on management of management training centres.* Brussels, Belgium: EFMD Publications.

EFMD. (1990). *EFMD guide to MBA programmes.* Brussels, Belgium: EFMD Publications.

EFMD. (1996). *Training the fire brigade: Preparing for the unimaginable.* Brussels, Belgium: EFMD Publications.

EFMD. (2008). *EFMD/GMAC corporate recruiters report.* Brussels, Belgium: EFMD Publications.

EFMD. (2012). *EFMD draft manifesto for management education.* Brussels, Belgium: EFMD Publications.

Fragueiro, F., & Thomas, H. (2011). *Strategic leadership in the business school: Keeping one step ahead.* Cambridge, UK: Cambridge University Press.

Ghoshal, S. (2005). Bad management theories are destroying good management practices. *Academy of Management Learning and Education, 4*(1), 75–91.

Grey, C. (2005). Chapter 5. In *A very short, interesting and reasonably cheap book about studying organisations.* London: Sage.

Hamel, G. (1996). P. 113 in EFMD (1996) (op. cit.).

Handy, C. B. (1996). Pp. 11 and 208 in EFMD (1996) (op. cit.).

Hubert, T. (1996). Pp. 27–29 in EFMD (1996) (op. cit.).

Iniguez, S. (2011). *The learning curve.* London: Palgrave Macmillan.

Jacobs, M. (2009). How business schools have failed business. *Wall Street Journal* (Eastern edition), April 24, p. A13.

Kerr, S. (1975). Folly of rewarding A, while hoping for B. *Academy of Management Journal, 18*(4), 769–783.

Khurana, R. (2007). *From higher aims to hired hands: The social transformation of American business schools and the unfulfilled promise of management as a profession*. Princeton, NJ: Princeton University Press.

Locke, E. R., & Spender, J. C. (2011). *Confronting managerialism*. London: Zed Books.

Lorange, P. (1996). Pp. 141–142 in EFMD (1996) (op. cit.).

March, J. G., & Simon, H. A. (1958). *Organisations*. New York, NY: Wiley.

Meltzer, A. P. (2012). *Why capitalism?* Oxford: Oxford University Press.

Mintzberg, H. (2004). *Managers not MBAs*. Harlow: Pearson Education.

Mintzberg, H. (2007). *Tracking strategies: toward a general theory*. Oxford: Oxford University Press.

Mintzberg, H. (2009). *Managers not MBAs: A hard look at the soft practice of managing and management development*. San Francisco, CA: Berrelt Koehler Publishers.

Moldoveanu, M. C., & Martin, R. (2008). *The future of the MBA*. Oxford: Oxford University Press.

Noorda, S. (2011). Future business schools. *Journal of Management Development*, *30*(5), 519–525.

Nueno, P. (1996). P. 55 in EFMD (1996) (op. cit.).

Nussbaum, M. C. (1997). *Cultivating humanity: A classical defense of reform in liberal education*. Cambridge, MA: Harvard University Press.

Osbaldeston, M. (1996). Pp. 215–216 in EFMD (1996) (op. cit.).

Pfeffer, J., & Fong, C. T. (2002). The end of business schools? Less success than meets the eye. *Academy of Management: Learning and Education*, *1*(1), 79–95.

Prahalad, C. K. (1996). P. 109 in EFMD (1996) (op. cit.).

Rameau, C. (1996). P. 57 in EFMD (1996) (op. cit.).

Schlegelmilch, B. B., & Thomas, H. (2011). The MBA in 2020: Will there still be one. *Journal of Management Development*, *30*(5), 474–482.

Thomas, H. (2012). What is the European management school model? *Global Focus*, *6*(1), 18–21.

Thomas, H., & Wilson, A. D. (2011). Physics envy, cognitive legitimacy or practical relevance: Dilemmas in the evolution of management research in the U.K. *British Journal of Management*, *22*, 443–456.

Van Schaik, R. (1996). P. 14 in EFMD (1996) (op. cit.).

Zingales, L. (2012). *A capitalism for the people: Recapturing the lost genius of American prosperity*. New York, NY: Basic Books.

Appendix

List of Respondents: Alphabetically

Name	Title
Christoph Badelt	Rector, WU (Vienna), Austria
George Bickerstaffe	Consultant Editor, Global Focus and founding editor of Which MBA, Economist, UK
Della Bradshaw	Management Editor, Financial Times, UK
Jordi Canals	Dean, IESE, Barcelona, Spain
Carlos Cavalle	Entrepreneur and Former Dean, IESE, Barcelona, Spain
Dan Le Clair	COO, AACSB International, USA
Eric Corneul	Director General and CEO, EFMD, Belgium
Sue Cox	Dean, Lancaster University Management School, UK
Rolf Cremer	President, European Business School, Frankfurt and Former Dean, CEIBS Business School, Shanghai, China
Arnoud de Meyer	President, Singapore Management University, Singapore and Former Dean, Cambridge Judge Business School, University of Cambridge, UK & Deputy Dean, INSEAD, France
John Fernandes	President and CEO, AACSB International, USA
James Fleck	Former Dean, Open University Business School, UK
Thierry Grange	Dean, Grenoble Ecole Du Management, France
Chris Greensted	Associate Director, Quality Services, EFMD, UK
Jim Herbolich	Director, Network Services, EFMD (Deceased)
Frank Horwitz	Director, Cranfield Business School, UK Formerly Director, Graduate School of Business, University of Cape Town, South Africa
Mike Jones	Director, Foundation for Management Education, UK

Appendix (*Continued*)

Name	Title
John Kraft	Dean, University of Florida, USA
Peter Lorange	President, Lorange Institute of Business, Zurich, Switzerland
Xavier Mendoza	Deputy Director, ESADE, Barcelona, Spain
Dave Montgomery	Distinguished Professor of Marketing, Stanford University, CA, USA
Michel Patry	President, HEC Montreal, Quebec, Canada
Kai Peters	CEO, Ashridge Management College, UK
John Peters	Senior Partner, GSE Research, UK
Liliana Petrella	Director, Development Initiatives, EFMD, Belgium
Martine Plompen	Associate Director, Research & Surveys Unit, EFMD, Belgium
Bill Russell	Director of Marketing, Emerald Publishing, UK
Thomas Sattleberger	Vice-President, EFMD former Board Member, Deutsche Telekom, Germany
David Saunders	Dean, Queens University Business School, Ontario, Canada
Julio Urgel	Deputy Director General, Operations and Quality, EFMD, Belgium
Ray Van Schaik	Honorary President, EFMD, Brussels; Retired CEO, Heineken
Stephen Watson	European Representative, AACSB International, Cambridge Univ, UK
	Formerly Director of Judge Business School, Cambridge University, UK
Robin Wensley	Professor of Management, Warwick Business School and Director of Advanced Institute of Management (AIM), UK
Greg Whittred	Dean, University of Auckland Business School, New Zealand
David Wilson	President and CEO, GMAC, USA
David Wilson	Head of Sociology, Warwick Business School, Univ. of Warwick, UK
Matthew Wood	Director of Communication, EFMD, Belgium
Zihong Yi	Dean, Renmin Univ Business School, China
Phil Zerillo	Professor, SMU and Chairman of Advisory Board of MIM, Thammasat University, Thailand

Afterword: The Past and Changes Needed in the Future

So there is Volume 1. It provides a rich array of evidence on where management education now stands — its strengths, weaknesses, challenges and lessons learned and not learned.

Volume 2 focuses on what our interviewees perceive as the challenges facing management education. If Volume 1 dissected the past, Volume 2 is about assembling the future, or at least a perception of what the future might possibly be like. It will certainly present management education with a changed environment and require the industry to confront change and adapt strategically in response.

To do this, Volume 2:

- First, considers how to address the blind spots, the unfulfilled promises and lessons left unlearned in management education.
- Second, it discusses alternative models and scenarios for business schools and addresses concerns about the mission/purpose of the business school.
- Third, it examines conjectures about the future and the challenges facing the leaders of business schools.
- Fourth, it provides a framework, and an agenda, for future growth.

Volume 2 will be published later this year.